PARRACOMBE
AND THE HEDDON VALLEY

AN UNFINISHED HISTORY

Published by
Parracombe Archaeology & History Society

ISBN 978-1-8384822-1-3

Compiled by Karen Farrington
Edited by Nick Constable
Contributors: June Aiken, Brian Barrow, David Blackmore, Linda Blanchard, Sally Chapman-Walker, Teresa Councell, Terry Green, Phil Griffiths, Julia Holtom, David Lear, Stewart Yeo

With special thanks to: Marjorie Bray, Steve Chope. Dr Peter Claughton, Gwen Dallyn, Bill Delbridge, Pam Latham, Brian Moore, Audrey Petherick, Philip Petherick, John Petherick snr, John Petherick jnr, John Roberts, Rosie Rogers, Molly Smyth, Ada Tucker, Mike Warburton, Annie York, Liz Rodway, Jill Le Dieu, Gary Marsh and 'Awards for All'

Picture research by June Aiken
Designed by Bruce Aiken

Pictures: To all those who brought their pictures to be scanned and stored in the PAHS archive we owe a special debt of thanks. All the images in this book, plus many more, are now recorded along with relevant information about them. This archive is an ongoing project and more pictures will certainly be appreciated for any further editions of this book.

Published sources:
The History of Parracombe (c. 1876) Arthur Smyth
The Field Archaeology of Exmoor; Hazel Riley and Robert Wilson-North (2001)
Archaeology of Exmoor; L V Grinsell (1970)
A Gazetter of British Lower and Middle Palaeolithic Sites; D A Roe (1968)
A List of Mines in North Devon & West Somerset; Dr Peter Claughton
The Mining Journal
The North Devon Journal
Exmoor Review
Redundant Churches Fund Guide of St Petrock's
The Heritage of Exmoor by Roger A Burton
Blackmores of Parracombe: Letters of Reuben Blackmore
Parracombe: Henry Blackmore's Memoir
Blackmores of Parracombe: A Family of Thirteen at Court Place
Blackmores of Parracombe: Some Black Sheep?
(all Blackmore books published by David Blackmore of Blackmore Books, Coniston, Newton Lane, Chester CH2 2HJ)

Contents

Introduction

The car maker Henry Ford once observed that 'all history is bunk' and in one sense he had a point. History is never an absolute truth because it is tarnished by prejudice, assumptions, mistakes and conflicting points of view. It also suffers from frustrating gaps (usually just as things get really interesting) and the familiar jibe that a particular event is reported 'out of context'.

In writing this book the Parracombe Archaeological and History Society (PAHS) is acutely aware of all these pitfalls - and plenty more. For one thing we've tried to condense some 300,000 years of human activity into a few short chapters. It's fair to say we might have missed the odd bit out!

Secondly, and despite our best efforts to publicise our research, there must be literally thousands of documents, deeds, letters and photos still lying out there undiscovered. No doubt some will say 'why on earth didn't they include so-and-so', to which the frank answer will almost certainly be 'because no-one told us'. Very little, if any, of the information supplied by local people has been rejected.

And of course very many local people did give up their time to help with research, did donate yellowing photos and dusty parchments and did suggest lines of inquiry or interviewees. There is a full list of acknowledgements at the back but to everyone who made this book happen PAHS owes a big vote of thanks. We are proud that this is a genuine community effort - about, by and for Parracombe people.

We also send special thanks to those nice people at Awards For All who have covered the cost of printing and publishing. It should be stressed that nobody, other than the printer, has been paid or received any expenses for their work on the book.

So, what will you find inside? Although some of the material has been published elsewhere a great deal is new and original and we hope everyone will discover at least something they didn't know. Generally speaking, chapters are organised by subject rather than chronologically - the idea being that you can dip in and out without having to read everything from the start.

There is some fascinating detail on everything from early farm accounts to church ledgers, school punishment records to raucous goings-on at Revels. But the real meat of the book lies in its characters and people; their hopes, fears, triumphs and tragedies. We meet the churchgoer who enjoyed having his foot kissed, the Sunday School preacher almost set alight by pupils, the schoolteacher who froze to death in a snowstorm, the lovelorn farmer who drowned himself, the aged resident whose coffin was carried aloft for three miles, the men behind Parracombe's long-lost silver mine, the farmers who fought rat and cockroach invasions, the postmaster who arrested a German bomber pilot, survival stories from the Lynmouth Flood - all these and many more human tales lie within.

The book also pulls together perhaps the most definitive single account yet of Parracombe's war dead, charting the fate of the young servicemen who left the peace and beauty of this corner of Devon for

From a postcard sent in February 1906. Before electricity poles, telephone cables, bungalows and modern houses - but otherwise practically unchanged.

the carnage of Europe's great 20th century battlefields. Their names appear on various village gravestones and the war memorial - now at last we can learn something of their lives.

PAHS accepts total responsibility for any errors or omissions and would welcome any constructive criticism. We'd also like to see any new material which might shed light on the events described or which reveal hitherto unknown aspects of the village's past. If you think you have a historical gem lurking in some dark drawer or cupboard please contact the Society on 01598 763296

It's worth remembering that the history in these pages belongs to all of us, whether we've lived here nine days or ninety years. It is dedicated to everyone who loves the village, cherishes its past and cares for its future. But mostly, to those who made Parracombe what it is.

PAHS, April 2004

1 Early Days

Parracombe, in its sheltered and fertile vale, distinguished itself by the sheer number of its farms - hence its Anglo-Saxon name pearoc cumbe, 'valley of the enclosures'.

The recent discovery of a pot dating from the Bronze or Early Iron Age was made at an archaeological dig at Holworthy Farm.

The very first visitors to what we now call the Heddon Valley lived some 300,000 years ago during the early Stone Age. A handaxe found 15 miles up the coast at Porlock, Somerset, is the earliest evidence of human activity on Exmoor but archaeologists actually know very little about how these people lived. Most likely they were nomadic scavengers who used flimsy camps or crude windbreaks for shelter. They would have known the secret of fire but were some way from being effective hunters.

The last major Ice Age began around 30,000 years ago at a time when northern Europe and Britain were joined together. Hunting communities would certainly have been operating on Exmoor at this time but when the ice mass reached its peak (18,000 - 11,500 BC) the entire country must have been all but uninhabitable. It wasn't until the Mesolithic period (10,000 - 4,000 BC) that hunter-gatherer people began returning to Exmoor and a warmer climate allowed arctic landscapes to become woodland. This in turn brought a greater variety of food and a demand for new stone hunting tools.

Hunter-gatherer communities were small - perhaps ten men and thirty women and children - and highly mobile. They would have been self-sufficient in basic foodstuffs for most of the year although food and other commodities were shared or exchanged with other groups. Before about 6,000 BC there would have been little in the way of woodland or vegetation in southwest Britain and therefore not many animals. It is possible the entire peninsular supported a population of less than 100 people, ie only 2 or 3 bands.

Neolithic (Stone Age) tools have been found near Parracombe at Kentisbury Down and in the mid-1960s around 600 shaped flints, probably arrow, spear or harpoon heads, were recovered from a ploughed field by the Rev. W G Eyre, Rector of Kentisbury. By Neolithic times - between 4000 and 2000 BC - early farmers would certainly have occupied the area and a disc-shaped flint knife from this period found on Kentisbury Common can be seen in the Museum of Barnstaple and North Devon.

One truly exciting find - made in 2003 - was recorded by the North Devon Archaeological Society during excavations at Holworthy Farm, south of the village. Volunteers unearthed the remains of a pot apparently dating from the Bronze or Early Iron Age and thought to be at least as early as 500 BC. Once conservation work is complete it will go on show at the Museum of Barnstaple and North Devon. At the time of writing further excavations are planned at this site in conjunction with Exeter University.

By the Bronze Age (c 2000 - 700 BC) the hills around Parracombe would have been a veritable buzz of activity and the resulting landscape has never, so far as we can tell, undergone large-scale re-organisation. The pattern of settlements, trackways, fields and field-boundaries around the village therefore reflects a piecemeal colonisation of the land by farmers, builders and industrialists over thousands of years.

There is no shortage of clues - Bronze Age barrows, standing stones, Iron Age enclosures, a Roman signal station, a memorial stone inscribed in Latin, an ancient church, a Norman castle mound, a deserted medieval settlement, two silver mines, a quarry and an abandoned railway - all relics that shaped the landscape of Parracombe and its neighbouring parishes of Martinhoe, Challacombe, Trentishoe and Lynton.

Among the area's best known prehistoric landmarks are the Chapman Barrows, burial mounds dating from the second millennium BC. The nine main barrows, each more than 20 metres in diameter, form an elongated cemetery which follows the southeast axis of a hill (perhaps a tribal boundary far older than the barrows themselves). To the southeast is the fine Longstone Barrow and, still further east, Wood Barrow on the county boundary - later used as a perimeter marker for the Royal Forest of Exmoor.

The dramatic setting of these mounds on the high moor, close to the parish boundary between Challacombe and Parracombe, has long been associated with stories of magic and mystery. In 1630 Thomas Westcote wrote how 'fiery dragons have been seen flying and lighting on them'. Westcote also tells how, when one of the barrows was opened by treasure hunters, a large 'brass pan' was recovered; possibly the remains of a bronze vessel.

In 1885 The Rev John Frederick Chanter, Rector of Parracombe and a keen amateur archaeologist, discovered that a village labourer had been ordered by a farmer to remove stones from one of the Chapman Barrows to build a hedge bank. The man, Thomas Antell, reported finding a 2ft square flat stone slab beneath which was a 2ft high by 1ft 6in wide pot containing burnt bones.

Antell claimed these were sheep bones, although human cremation seems more likely. Ten years later Chanter himself opened the easternmost barrow and discovered a central burial pit, topped with stone slabs and a cairn. Bones and teeth were identified in the cremated material and a large amount of charcoal was present.

Arguably Exmoor's single best-known Bronze Age landmark is the Longstone. This 9ft high slate monolith is located some 750 yards to the southeast of the main Chapman Barrows line and is surprisingly slim (around seven inches thick). Anyone who has walked alone in this wild and beautiful setting amid the gathering gloom of a winter's evening will know something of the magical atmosphere it generates.

Recent discoveries about ancient iron smelting at Brayford are fast re-writing the area's Iron Age

The Longstone at Chapman Barrows - a 9ft high Bronze Age monolith.

The excavated central burial pit of one of Chapman Barrows' burial mounds

history. In short, there's much more of it than anyone realised! Around Parracombe the roughly circular earth-banked enclosures at Voley and Beacon Hill are thought to date from this period (500BC - AD45) but are still to be examined closely. In 2002 a similar enclosure at Holworthy (near the bronze pot site - see above) was partly excavated by the North Devon Archaeological Society and work is ongoing to find clear dating evidence. One thing is becoming clearer: not all these earthworks were 'castles' or 'camps' as some old maps suggest but rather farmsteads and animal enclosures.

An earth banked enclosure at Voley, thought to date between 500BC to AD45, is yet to reveal any secrets.

War in the West

The Romans came to Parracombe around the middle of the first century AD, as they tightened their grip on southwest Britain. For many years it was thought they had little interest in Devon and Cornwall and even up until the 1970s there was a general belief that their western push ended at Bath. Exeter was thought to have been a minor civilian settlement while Cornwall was regarded as a Celtic stronghold free of Roman interference.

Recent archaeology has turned all this on its head, proving that history never lies quietly in dust-covered textbooks! We now know that Exeter was a major military garrison following Emperor Claudius's AD43 invasion and became the operational base for the entire Second Legion. Although the Army later re-located to Caerleon, in South Wales, to deal with the troublesome Silures tribe, Exeter remained a Roman colony for at least 350 years - right into the twilight of the Empire. North Devon was certainly drawn into the economy of Roman Britain, as illustrated by the exciting recent discovery of extensive iron workings at Brayford.

It is thought a Roman fortlet or signal station at Martinhoe, excavated by Lady Aileen Fox and Professor Ravenhill in the 1960s, was built partly to monitor Silures activity in the Bristol Channel. It was probably occupied by troops of the Second Legion between AD55 and AD75 and is identical to an earlier Channel lookout post - Old Burrow near County Gate - which it apparently replaced.

Old Burrow was manned for perhaps five years and was never more than a temporary outpost, relying heavily on local food suppliers. There's no evidence of buildings so we must assume the soldiers lived in tents, a thankless posting on stormy winter nights. In comparison Martinhoe was positively luxurious with timber buildings around a small courtyard, ovens and a forge. Judging by the amount of native pottery unearthed Roman troops here had a healthy working relationship with the locals.

Following the collapse of the Empire in the early 5th century AD historical fact and fiction tend to merge. However near Parracombe we do have one reassuringly solid relic in the shape of the Cavudus stone, a memorial slab etched with a 5th century Latin script which in 1913 was found serving as a gatepost near Caffyns Cross (it now stands in private ground at Six Acre Farm). The inscription CAVUDI FILIUS CIVILIS - '(the grave of) Cavudus, son of

Civilis' is early Celtic Christian in style and is similar to inscribed stones elsewhere in the South-West, including Lundy Island and Winsford Hill.

The Dark Ages - that period between the end of Roman rule and the arrival of the Normans - are truly dark so far as Parracombe is concerned. From what little is known it seems the village was part of the Kingdom of Dumnonia, an amalgamation of smaller fiefdoms which covered Cornwall, Devon and West Somerset. Parracombe stood just 30 miles from the eastern border.

The origins of the Dumnonii are unknown and as they left precious few written records, and no coinage (they preferred to barter goods), their political and economic systems remain a mystery. It seems aristocratic lineage and honour were of great importance to this isolated tribe but, to date, barely a handful of their kings have been identified. History has grudgingly yielded names such as Constantine, Cadwy and Geraint and there's some evidence that Dumnonia was known to other British kingdoms as 'the Land of the Western Welsh'.

The dedication of Parracombe's old parish church to St Petrock supports the idea of close cultural contacts with Welsh tribes. It bears the mark of Celtic Christians and mirrors similar dedications to St Brannock at Braunton, St Kea at Landkey, St Brendan at Brendon and St Dubricius at Porlock. Missionaries from South Wales were certainly active along the North Devon and Somerset coasts in the early medieval period and it's fair to assume that they left church dedications in key communities where local leaders regarded a Christian presence as useful. Among these, Parracombe, in its sheltered and fertile valley, distinguished itself by the sheer number of its farms - hence its Anglo-Saxon name *pearoc cumbe*, 'valley of the enclosures'.

Terms such as 'Celtic' Christian need a brief explanation as there has been much heart-searching among archaeologists over what 'Celtic' actually *means*. In this case it refers to the early, pre-Augustinian Church in Britain, which probably had its roots in the Roman period and was particularly influential where British culture and language survived (ie in western Britain). This branch of Christianity was characterised by monasticism, a reverence for wild places, an earthy, poetic delight in 'nature' and an independence which put the 'Celtic' church at loggerheads with the authoritarian Roman church forged by St Ambrose and championed by Augustine. It threw up numerous local 'saints', principal among whom was St Dyfrig or Dubricius to whom Porlock church is dedicated.

The last of Dumnonia's kings probably ruled in the 9th century AD, their influence eclipsed by advancing Anglo-Saxon tribes. However it would be wrong to think of this as a 'conquest' in the accepted sense. For perhaps 300 years there would have been a gradual shift towards the Saxon language and culture - a process hastened by the long term emigration of Dumnonii people to Brittany.

The late ninth century, and the arrival of the Vikings, must have been a fearful time for exposed coastal communities such as Parracombe. The Anglo-Saxon Chronicle tells how, in AD 851, Ceorl and his kin of Devon defeated the Danes near Torbay and in AD 878 an unidentified brother of Ivar the Boneless and Halfden crossed the Bristol Channel to launch an attack on the North Devon coast at a place called Arx Cynuit. According to one theory this is modern-day Countisbury although there are problems in linking the two names. Whatever the precise location, a great battle was fought within a few miles of Parracombe in which the Vikings suffered huge losses of perhaps 800 warriors. One plausible idea is that the defenders re-occupied the substantial ancient earthwork at Wind Hill, above Sillery Sands, Countisbury. Until the site is properly excavated to prove a 9th century re-use this must remain conjecture.

Norman Conquest

In 1066, William of Normandy invaded and conquered England resulting in the construction of

Norman fortresses across the country. Holwell Castle at Parracombe - comparable to similar garrisons at Barnstaple and Bampton - is among the best preserved of its type and size, with traces of buildings in the bailey clearly visible.

The motte or mound and its bailey enclosure date from the later 11th century and lie close to a bridging point on the River Heddon. The site was probably chosen to control movement through the valley and around it medieval Parracombe took shape, the castle's presence perhaps attracting settlement away from the hamlets at Churchtown, Bodley, Middleton and Rowley.

To the south of the castle at Higher Holwell was another settlement, now visible only as earthworks. Here aerial photography has revealed the remnants of ridge and furrow ploughing (best seen in low winter sunlight) and it's clear that the deserted village lies among the furlongs of a medieval common field. Similar patterns can be seen to the north of Bodley and it seems Parracombe was surrounded by intensive medieval arable farming.

If these ancient plough marks are traced onto a modern map of the area, with its numerous irregular fields and boundaries, it becomes clear that many existing boundaries must be very old, since either they respect the ridge and furrow or the ridge and furrow respects them!

Historically, arable farming demanded much more land than it does today and careful examination of the field-boundaries around Parracombe suggests a history of arable expansion and gradual encroachment onto common grazing. Mixed farming communities needed fertile land close at hand for their crops so animals were generally grazed further afield. However animal dung was the main practical means of maintaining soil fertility. The movement of animals therefore had to be closely controlled so that growing crops wouldn't be trampled and dung could be conveniently collected and deposited where it was needed.

Enclosing an area of ground to be intensively cultivated and manured created an 'infield'. Today these early enclosures can be detected in well-preserved field patterns, acting as focal points around which other systems developed. In

The motte and bailey of Holwell Castle, extremely well preserved. A Norman construction dating from the latter half of the 11th century.

Parracombe there are two candidates, at Bodley and Churchtown. Both are quite clear on the tithe map of 1842 and it's still possible to walk round much of the Churchtown enclosure on footpaths. The enclosing hedge bank remains very substantial and stockproof.

In some medieval communities a long barrier between the Common Moor and arable land helped keep the 'horn' from the corn. In Parracombe two such boundaries can be detected. One runs from Ley's Lane towards Minniemoor Cross and then south towards Rowley, its long, curving boundary clearly visible on a modern 1:25000 map.

The second sweeps around from Bodley to East Hill and is best observed on the 1842 tithe map. The likely function of these boundaries is revealed by the names associated with them: on the one hand Minniemoor; on the other the field names Meana Ground and Mince's Ground (both near Bodley). All these names contain the Anglo-Saxon element *(ge)mœne(s)*, meaning 'common' or 'Common Moor', suggesting they once marked the edge of the Common.

As Parracombe's medieval farmers extended their activities, enclosing and ploughing more of the Common, they created long, slightly curving strips known as selions. When farming practice changed, blocks of selions were enclosed to make fields, their curvature lingering on in the alignment of hedge-banks. This arrangement is very obvious at Kemacott and Heale but also features within the parish, especially in the pattern of parallel, gently curving boundaries between east Middleton and Rowley.

The final phase of enclosure was a very different affair; Parliamentary Inclosure in the later 19th and early 20th centuries imposed straight field boundaries on an otherwise organic landscape and these can be seen on the edge of the high moor at Parracombe Common.

While Bronze Age barrows and Roman or Norman forts are obvious to the eye, the archaeology of field-patterns is more subtle. Yet these ancient boundaries, which represented such a big investment of rural manpower, are important monuments to the men and women who laboured to create them. They were made to last and any bank around two metres high and three metres at the base is probably the original article. Another telltale clue is the appearance of a mixed deciduous hedge on top of the bank, together with old stools of ash and oak.

A medieval 'corn ditch' intended to keep the stock animals from the cereal crops.

2 The Making of a Village

'The populace would meet at the Royal Hotel, then known as the London Inn, and having got decently drunk they would proceed to business.'

According to White's Devonshire Directory of 1878, the manor of Parracombe was granted by William I to his associate William de Falaise, a comrade-at-arms during the Battle of Hastings. It was only one of numerous holdings awarded to this Norman nobleman and no one knows if he actually visited in person. The land was previously owned by a Saxon chieftain called Beorhtwald.

It is assumed that Falaise, or perhaps his heir Robert Fitzmartin, built the Norman motte and bailey castle to guard a junction of east-west and north-south trade routes. Even so, it's remarkable that Parracombe should have been chosen for fortification ahead of larger communities such as Combe Martin.

The name Holwell Castle derives from the structure's close proximity to three holy wells, although only two are marked on maps. One was called Holy Well although its exact location isn't known. The other two - St Thomas's Well and Lady's Well - are in the vicinity of Churchtown.

There are no records relating to the castle in its heyday but defensive timber walls and a one or two storey wooden shelter probably topped the earthworks. Almost certainly it was operational for only a short spell.

The Domesday Book says Falaise held Parracombe - or Parrecumb - in 1086. The hamlet, one manor among several locally, paid tax for half a hide (about 60 acres) and had a taxable population of five villagers and eight smallholders. Only the heads of households were counted so this number didn't include wives, children and slaves. There were also 10 cattle, 27 sheep and 27 goats.

Parracombe was just one manor among several in the locality. Rowley, which is separately mentioned, was a smaller community with three villagers and two smallholders. Like neighbouring Middleton, the manor was held by Geoffrey of Mowbray, the Bishop of Coutances in France. Loyal to William I, Geoffrey was implicated in the rebellion against his successor William Rufus although he was pardoned for his role.

When Geoffrey died in 1098 his fief passed to his nephew Robert of Mowbray, Earl of Northumberland, who ironically was then compelled to forfeit it as a penalty for his role in the rebellion against William Rufus. Middleton belonged to Iudhael of Totnes, then his son Alfred. It was bequeathed to a sister who married Henry de Tracey.

Likewise, Parracombe descended through the Fitzmartin family to the Traceys, the barons of Barnstaple at the time of Edward I. Ultimately it fell to the St Albyns who held it until 1860 when Langley St Albyn gave up his manorial rights.

By now the three manors considered part of Parracombe were Middleton, formerly called Midland, owned by William Dovell; Court Place owned by Charles Blackmore jnr. and Rowley, belonging to John Nott-Pyke. Nott-Pyke's uncle bought the property from one Mrs Roach, the heir to the Lock family.

Life in medieval times remains something of a mystery although there is some reliable information about the mills in and around Parracombe. Here we

Parracombe Mill - the only mill wheel still turning in the parish.

list some of them, beginning in the upper reaches of the River Heddon and heading downstream.

Highley. This mill was originally on land owned by Pilton Priory but when the priory was dissolved in 1536 it was taken over by King Henry VIII who subsequently allocated the land in grants. There is a contemporary reference to Highley being 'A tenement with mill, fishery, weir and lands in Highley held by John Quycke'.

Tucking Mill. Known as 'Tokynmyll' in 1543, when it was run by one John Thorne. Tucking is a term for the finishing process that cleans and felts woven cloth. There's a suggestion that a horse was once harnessed here to a capstan bar that turned a heavy roller to provide power. The mill was later owned by local MP Sir Thomas Acland and the site was eventually converted into two homes for labourers. It is now better known as Sunnyside Farm.

Parracombe Mill. Described as a Fulling Mill in 1543, which means it was used in the production of cloth. The power from the water wheel was geared to raise large wooden mallets that pounded the cloth in troughs filled with fullers earth and water, a process designed to thicken the material. Later the building was used for milling grain.

Bumsley Mill. A sale here advertised in the North Devon Journal in 1861 describes two pairs of stones (one French, one Welsh), a good flour machine with sufficient gear for working the same and a pond with a never-failing stream of water.

Milltown, **Millwood** or **Mill Farm**. A little downstream from Bumsley it was built around 1500.

Tucking Mill. Lying further down the valley and presumably used for cloth making.

Millham or **Mill Ham**. The last of the Heddon mills (going downstream) in Parracombe it was sited close to the parish boundary, opposite The Barton.

There were also at least two spring or leat-fed mills which were:

Rowley Barton. Records show that its wheel (made by S T Born of Milltown, Marwood) was 14ft 6 ins (5.3 metres) in diameter, 3 ft wide and bore 48 oak buckets. The rim gear contained 372 teeth and had cast iron cogs at the side that engaged with a second gear connected to a short shaft and nine-inch bevel wheel. This turned an overhead shaft that ran to the large granary.

The mill worked well enough until 1925 when a new owner came to the farm and used an engine instead. Like any grain store, mills would at times have been serious fire risks and indeed one blaze reduced Trentishoe Mill to a pile of rubble.

Middleton. Records show that as long ago as 1249 there was a mill at Middleton (given to John de Weston and his wife Joan by Walter Beghel). But this may have in fact been a reference to the mill at Voley. The North Devon Journal of 11th July 1930 gives details of its sale. 'Well built stone and slated farmhouse, with convenient outbuildings including barn with thresher, water wheel, granary etc.'

Although not actually used as a mill, a water wheel was installed at Woolhanger Manor in the later 19th century. It operated an organ in the octagonal music room and was later removed to Yorkshire.

Wall plaques reveal that stone buildings were put up during the medieval period, presumably marking construction, re-construction or extensions. There are three at East Bodley. The porch is dated 1638, the ceiling 1739 and the fireplace 1755. Few others are known to exist.

As to the daily lives of Parracombe folk there's precious little written information until the mid-19th century although Rev John Chanter believes the population was fluid and relatively wealthy. In the preface of 'Parracombe Baptisms, Marriage, Burials 1597-1836', published in 1917 he wrote: 'Very few families stayed more than four of five generations in the parish, and this tendency is still going on, and at the present day there are not more than three or four families residing in the parish who have been in it for more than five generations.'

This was, he notes, quite the opposite of what happened in most similar villages around Devon. He gave two reasons:

'One is that the early dismemberment of the manors brought in men of sufficient substance to purchase freehold farms and become yeomen; the second was the large extent of common land in the parish and the rights that pertained to it of grazing cattle on the royal forest of Exmoor, which was favourable to the labouring classes rising to the ranks first of small farmers and then being able to migrate to richer farms and lands than they could find in the hill country of the Devonshire parishes that lie on the western slopes of Exmoor.

'The enclosure of the commons *[ie when it was taken into private ownership]* which was so prevalent in the beginning of the 19th century, while it has brought much land into cultivation that before was of little value and has prevented the spread of 'scab' among the flocks, has also resulted in making the rise from the position of an agricultural labourer, which was easy before, much more difficult, as well as practically taking what belonged to all inhabitants and giving it to a few, viz., the landowners.

'Owing to this the population is more stationary now than in the 17th and 18th centuries. Owing to the sale of Exmoor Forest, the grazing rights, which belonged to all the parishes that lay in the purlieu (*environs*) of the forest, of which Parracombe was one, have also been lost.'

His records book offers a brief insight into Parracombe life. In 1600 there were seven baptisms, three marriages and three burials at St Petrock's. A century later there were seven baptisms, two marriages and three burials while in 1800 there were again seven baptisms and two marriages but only one burial.

At the beginning of the 19th century infant and premature death still occurred frequently. William Roach, 22, Maria Roach, 14, and Richard Roach, 11, all of Parracombe Mill, died during 1814. Twenty years later Charles Lancey, aged four, of Parracombe Mill, died in February, ten days after his one year old brother Joseph. (Parracombe Mill was the name of the mill and its immediate neighbourhood.) However, for those that survived childhood and its associated illnesses, it was not uncommon for people to live into their seventies and beyond in an era when life expectancy fell far short of that age. John Lancey, of Parracombe Mill, was 89 when he was buried on 20th March 1825. Mary Gammon, of Highley, was 85 when she died in 1834.

As for the content of their daily lives at this time, we know little, although one charming anecdote

The Royal Hotel, because of limited level standing for carriages, was ultimately unable to compete with the Fox & Goose.

survives. It dates to the beginning of the 19th century when villagers elected a mayor and corporation - not to generate red tape and bureaucracy but rather to poke fun at politicians of the day. Arthur Smyth in his Parracombe history of 1876 gives a flavour of the antics involved:

'The populace would meet at the Royal Hotel, then known as the London Inn [now London House], and having got decently drunk they would proceed to business. At its close they would form into a procession and the elected Mayor, either by virtue of his unsteadiness by this time or for the sake of occuping a post of honour, would be placed in a wheelbarrow. Thus they would go through the village. This would be kept up until the corporate body were too drunk to go any further and then a

The Fox & Goose in the 1890s with George Smyth standing on the left. Just discernable above the entrance is written 'TEA COFFEE AND MILK' - a pub, a hotel and an early coffee bar?

few of the sober ones would drive His Worship up to the Mill pond and tip him in.' Smyth goes on to explain that the custom of picking a mayor was dropped upon the death of one fellow who had frequently been elected.

Doone Country

It may well be that novelist Richard Doddridge Blackmore (1825-1900), author of 'Lorna Doone', was acquainted with the custom. Opinion remains divided over the strength of his connection with Parracombe but one newspaper source makes a definite link.

'Mr R D Blackmore, as a youth, spent much of his time at Parracombe fishing and shooting. He owned a small part of Hele wood rising on the east side of the Heddon valley and his name is on the register of voters for Parracombe. Probably he inherited his love of sport from his father who often came here coursing and once they caught a pure white hare, which was stuffed.'

The newspaper clipping is undated although it was published after the writer's death. The contributor may well have been Arthur Smyth.

A White's directory, dated 1850 and a census the following year, are the first really reliable and detailed records of Parracombe's past. The biggest household at the time was referred to as the Parsonage, presumably Heddon Hall, which was built in 1827 at a cost of £1,000. (It is also listed in some historical documents as The Rectory.) Whites notes that the Rector, John Pike, lived there with his wife Elizabeth and their sons James, aged six, and George, seven. The family was served by a butler, groom, cook, nurse, housemaid and kitchen maid.

William Watts, the headmaster, apparently lived at or by the school with his wife Agnes, a schoolmistress, and their children aged 13, 11 and nine. The family had moved to Parracombe from Berrynarbor although Agnes was originally from Lynton. Cottages opposite the school - some of which have since been demolished - were occupied by tradespeople including two carpenters, a dressmaker, a thatcher, a shoemaker and an agricultural labourer. One 47-year-old female resident is described on the census as a 'pauper idiot'!

Corn millers were William Howe and Richard Lovering. The shopkeeper was John Lancey, the butcher John Lock and the maltster John Lovering. The Revenue Officer was one K Mackenzie, the blacksmith Richard Tucker, the tailor James Whitefield and the three wheelwrights William Burden, Mr Hatton and John Tamlyn. The turnpike gate keeper was named as 65 year old Thomas Lock of Turnpike Gate.

At the London Inn the victualler (and baker) was Alfred Polkinghorne. Thanks to the notes of a diarist, preserved in the records, it's clear that this hostelry was trading as a public house in August 1852. The unknown writer stopped there for ale, bread and butter en route for Lynton. At the rival Fox & Goose John Somervill was landlord. In 1862 the police station, with its two cells, was built. It was a proud building for so small a village but, at the time, Lynton had no police station so it acted as a base for the district sergeant. Previously, cells at the Old Post Office were used for holding prisoners.

At about this time the Mill was occupied by Robert Blackmore, his wife Susan and their rapidly expanding family. Robert, their third child, was born in the village in 1855 as was Susan in 1858, Mary Grace in 1859, Walter in 1860 (although his place of birth is given as Hatherington in the 1881 census) and Bessie Ann in 1863. Master miller Blackmore fathered two other children before the family was complete.

One of their descendants, Stewart Yeo, has tracked the movements of various family members. Robert snr. and Susan were living on Lundy Island with Walter and Helena, the last born, at the time of the '81 census. Blackmore was apparently hind (assistant) to Rev. G Heaven. The Reverend's diary mentions Blackmore sporadically, and implies the sudden death of a daughter and the baptism of a 'Blackmore babe'. Robert Blackmore died on 19th January 1903 aged 83.

We don't know which daughter died but it seems Bessie Ann survived and worked as a servant at the Ebberly Arms Inn in Barnstaple. At least, a Betsey Blackmore born in Parracombe was listed there in the 1881 census. She married John Yeo who later became the licensee and then the owner of the public house. Following his death in 1902 Bessie Ann ran the Ebberley Arms. She had at least four children, one of whom was Stewart Yeo's grandfather. When her son's short-lived marriage broke up Bessie Ann brought up his two children as well, one being Yeo's father.

At some point, probably in the mid-Twenties, Bessie Anne moved with two of her children and two grandchildren to Haldene Terrace in Barnstaple, which she ran as a bed and breakfast establishment. Following the death of her son Albert in a motorcycle accident in 1929 she moved to Ebberly Farm and Dairy, run by another son William and his wife Ada. Bessie Ann died in Barnstaple on 22nd February 1941 at the age of 78.

In 1871 Parracombe had 366 residents (187 male and 179 female living in 76 houses on 4,363 acres of land), not so very different from the population today. Smyth's 1876 history of Parracombe gives the following illuminating description of a trip through the village in the late 19th century. Some spelling, grammar and vocabulary may seem a little strange!

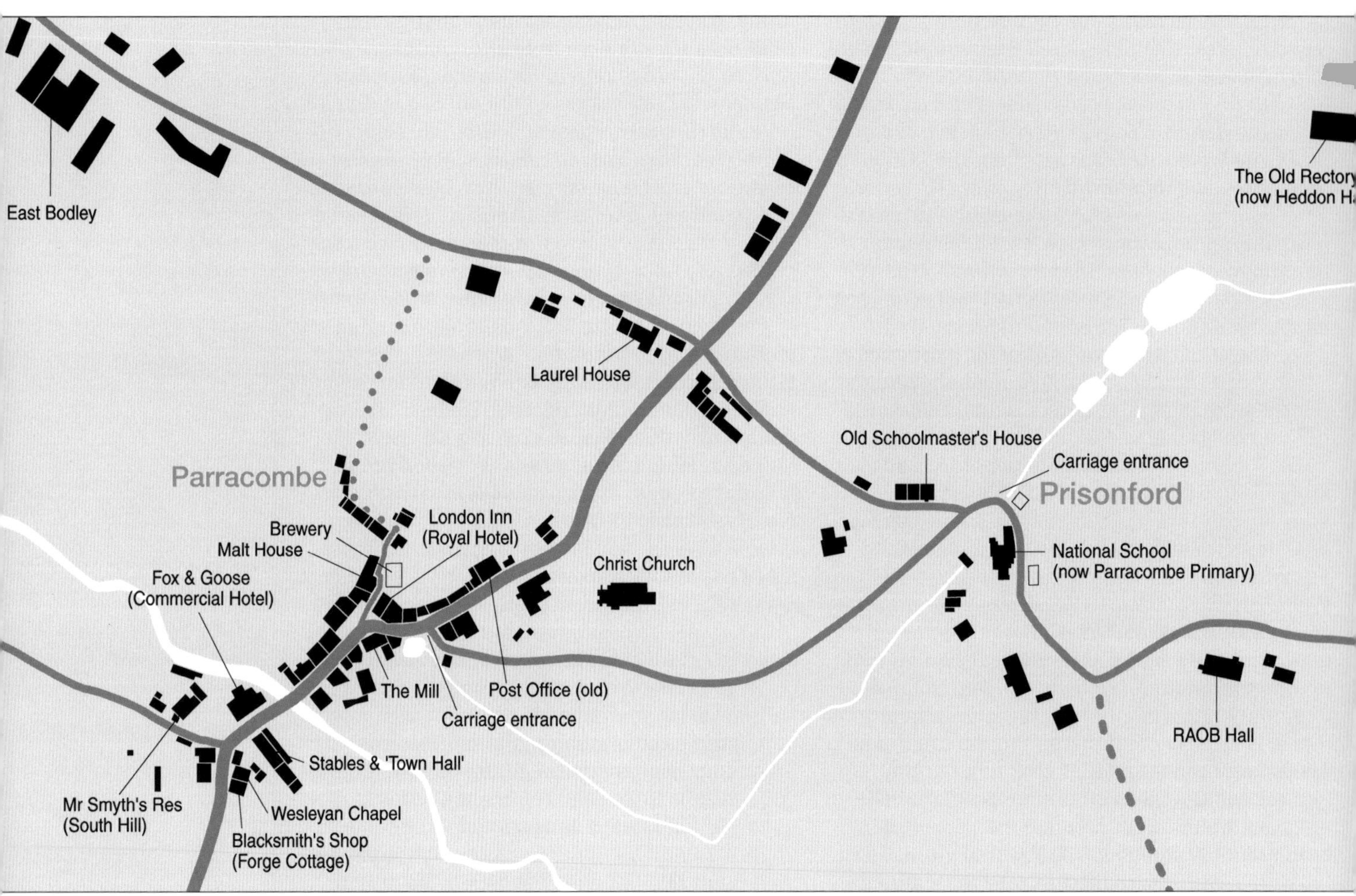

Parracombe circa 1950. Smyth's 1876 walk through the village can still be easily followed although some buildings are difficult to identify.

'On entering the village from Barnstaple side you find a few pretty cottages that have been built by the owner, Mr George Smyth, the Wesleyan Chapel and a blacksmith's shop adjoining one of them. Mr Smyth's residence lies at the foot of the hill, but surrounded with a high wall with large evergreen trees forming a screen makes the house very retired and quiet.

'Next is a public house, the Fox & Goose', that belongs to St Albyn who in 1859 sold it to Rev John Pyke whose son Mr I N P Nott now owns it. The dwelling house is very old and low but has been repaired at different times, some wings added so that now it is at least sound and fair size if not elegant. A new stable was built by Rev J Pyke with a large room over, which is called by courtesy the Town Hall.

'Close by runs the river that in winter time overflows and floods the Fox & Goose, this stream divides the Manors.

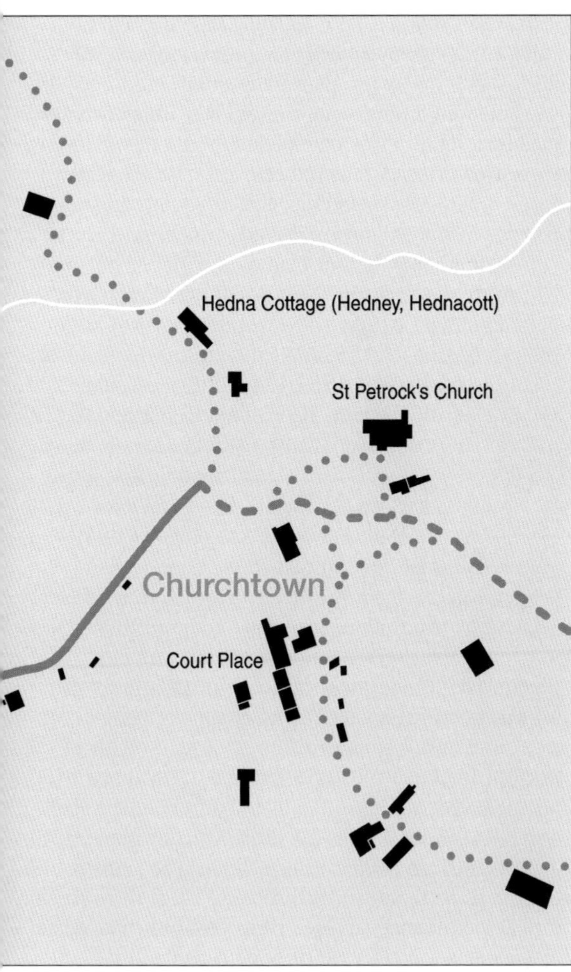

'Then, passing over the bridge directly in front of us is a very small, very low cottage, half thatch, half slate roof, one wall covered with ivy, this now belongs to one of the Rowley Roaches. Opposite is the house and offices of our worthy butcher who also keeps a general shop. It was built a few years ago by the present owner and occupied by Mr Daniel Gould. Next door is another cottage belonging to the Roaches. The front part seems modern.

'Next is a very old, small dilapidated affair, that belonged to the Hartons, now belongs to James Slader. Adjoining is rather a pretty cottage that has recently been altered and is now very convenient. It belongs as does the next cottage to Mr Richard Crocombe, Malster, Brewer etc. It has a very nice garden to the rear. Then comes the Malt-house built and owned years ago by the Loverings, and now does near the best business in the district. Opposite is the brewery built and opened last year and is well paying, these premises belonging to Mr Crocombe, the occupier. Beyond this lies the Terrace, containing a new cottage and three old thatched ones in a row. It now belongs to Mrs O Harding. Behind is another cottage belonging to Mr Crocombe.

Royal patronage

'Close by the Brewery is the London Inn. I beg pardon, I should say Royal Hotel for during the last tenant's resident the Prince of Wales [later Edward VII] called and had a glass of water, so they altered the sign in honour of the Royal visit. It is a modern house and has rather an imposing appearance but it does not do so good a business as the Fox & Goose, the standing for carriages is not so good being an incline. It belonged to the Loverings, now Mr Pyke Nott owns it.

'Opposite is the Mill, large and rambling concern very dilapidated but is under repair now. It belongs to the Loverings but is held under a life lease by Mr Blackmore of Laurel House.

'Next to the Royal Hotel is a cottage originally built for a bake house but it did not pay. It is now occupied by a shoemaker and belongs to Mr D Gould. Beyond is another cottage belonging to and occupied by Mary Wilkey, opposite is the carriage entrance to the Rectory and close by its gates on the south side is the Mill pond.

'On the North side is the post office and general shop built by the late Rev John Pyke, it is on the Glebe land, the shop is the largest and most imposing one in the village or parish. Opposite is a very small cottage and another larger one close to it, both were built by the late Mr Philip Dovell of Middleton, now they are the property of Mr Gould. The last house in the village is the police station and prison, rather a pretty frontage but is I believe rather small. It has but two cells which however are very seldom occupied.

'A few yards further up the hill is Bodley Cross, so called from four roadways meeting. One leads to Lynton, the other we came by, one to Bodley and the other to Prisonford and Court Place etc. Here is built a rather pretty house now called Laurel House, built and belonging to Mr Charles Blackmore snr. There is a general shop here conducted by the Misses Jones who also occupy part of the house, the other half is occupied by the owner. A little beyond on the Lynton road are two or three very old dilapidated cottages. I should scarcely fancy them habitable but they are occupied.

'Prisonford doubtless takes its name from the old prison being here in former days. . . . Whatever was the origin of its name, no trace of a prison is now visible. First we come to two very pretty small cottages built by the late Mr James Smyth of Bodley, now owned by his daughter Miss Elizabeth. Next door is a small dilapidated old cottage until lately used as a residence for the schoolmaster but since the late master's death the residence as aforementioned is at Hedney Cott. It is now used as a bake house, large ovens having recently been built. Miss Crocombe and her aged mother now occupy it, the former carrying on the business in which she is assisted by her brother who originated it but having lately married he now resides at Lynton.

'Now crossing the carriage entrance from the Rectory is another small old cottage which together with the last mentioned belong to Mr Pyke Nott. It is occupied by our rural postman, a bachelor who resides there alone, his name is Nathaniel Barwick, whose ancestors built and formerly owned the last-named cottage, it having been built on some waste land.

'Just beyond is a good-looking little cottage held under a lease from the owners of the Court Barton, and it was built by the present occupier and leasehold, John Somervill, mason. It is I believe very small inside but has a very pleasant aspect with a pretty view. Opposite is the National School, a low thatched building which has recently been enlarged by order of the Educational Department, and is now very commodious and well regulated. The present mistress has been here some few months now having been appointed at (gap). She has proved a most efficient mistress. *[Although the cottages opposite the school have long since disappeared there was an opportunity to excavate the site before the school car park was laid in 1996. Volunteers found a fire place, a bodley stove, bread oven, some leather from shoes, some nails, a bullet and some slate. It's known one belonged to a cobbler.Ed.].*

'Prisonford is situated just in the centre of the Glebe, a road passing through leading to Court Place, Church etc, the road bearing the name of Church Lane, in which there are three or four very old dilapidated cottages; the first is exceedingly small and was I believe one of the Manorial cottages purchased by the late Rev John Pyke of St Albyn, Lord of the Manor, before alluded to. It is very small and seems ready to tumble down, it is now and has been for some years occupied by William Spurrier, a labourer and attendant on fairs and revels with sweets, gingerbreads etc.

'A little further on stood a few years ago two cottages belonging to John Cornish and John Delbridge, the former's cottage is though small a convenient tidy little cottage occupied by Mr William Blackmore, who retired from Tucking Mill a few years ago. Delbridge's cottage having been left unoccupied very soon fell into decay and nothing can now be seen but a heap of stones. Just outside these cottages is a leaping stock, which I'm told was used years ago by Church people to mount their horses.

'Beyond in fact adjoining the Barton outbuildings is another small old cottage belonging like Spurrier's to Mr Pyke Nott and occupied by Robert Ralph. Church Lane is seldom used now by Church people, the Rectory forming a pleasant and better road, though the lane is still used for funerals and, of course, occupiers of farms lying in this neighbourhood.'

[Although he appears to have had no formal schooling Arthur Smyth became the literary character of the village, being author and newspaper correspondent. He was, by all accounts, a sickly child whose problems were exacerbated by the loss of an already lame leg, amputated in 1901. However, he fathered seven children: Frederick, who moved to London, Charles and Ernest, who both stayed in Parracombe, Edie, who married into the de Lancey family, Sissy, who moved to Launceston, Cornwall, Winnie, who moved to London, and Florrie who married postmaster Arthur Parkhouse. As a journalist it seems he was a constant thorn for both the parish and district councils. Before the end of the 19th century he acidly noted a parish council shortfall. 'No record of receipts and expenditure was produced although it was asked for, it being evident, as one gentleman remarked, that the parish council were rather reserved. However, let us hope for an improvement in this direction as a resolution was passed that their meetings in future shall be open to the public.' Again in 1898 he wrote: 'We read how in olden times the wise men came from the East. The councillors who recently came here to inspect our highways came from the West. They report Church Lane to be in bad condition, with sewerage running over it, nevertheless they do not advise the council to move in the matter but - herein they display their wisdom - should request the Railway Company to repair their part of the said road. That's it, do nothing yourself but keep others up to the mark.' In addition to writing he was known locally for his hand carvings and a large collection of birds' eggs. He died in 1935 and is buried at St Petrock's.- Ed.]

Court Place was apparently the home of the St Albyn family until it was sold to the Blackmores.

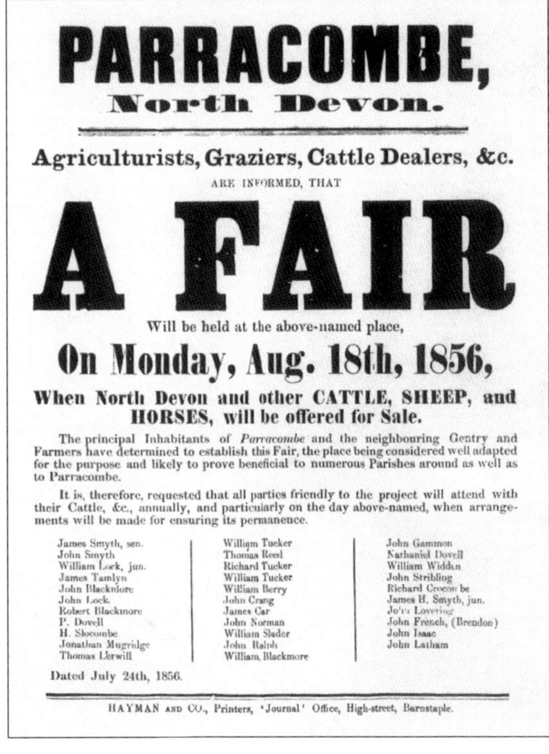

PARRACOMBE,
North Devon.

Agriculturists, Graziers, Cattle Dealers, &c.
ARE INFORMED, THAT

A FAIR

Will be held at the above-named place,

On Monday, Aug. 18th, 1856,

When North Devon and other CATTLE, SHEEP, and HORSES, will be offered for Sale.

The principal Inhabitants of *Parracombe* and the neighbouring Gentry and Farmers have determined to establish this Fair, the place being considered well adapted for the purpose and likely to prove beneficial to numerous Parishes around as well as to Parracombe.

It is, therefore, requested that all parties friendly to the project will attend with their Cattle, &c., annually, and particularly on the day above-named, when arrangements will be made for ensuring its permanence.

James Smyth, sen.	William Tucker	John Gammon
John Smyth	Thomas Reed	Nathaniel Dovell
William Lock, jun.	Richard Tucker	William Widden
James Tamlyn	William Tucker	John Stribling
John Blackmore	William Berry	Richard Crocombe
John Lock.	John Crang	James H. Smyth, jun.
Robert Blackmore	James Car	John Lovering
P. Dovell	John Norman	John French, (Brendon)
H. Slocombe	William Slader	John Isaac
Jonathan Mugridge	John Ralph	John Latham
Thomas Lerwill	William Blackmore	

Dated July 24th, 1856.

HAYMAN AND CO., Printers, 'Journal' Office, High-street, Barnstaple.

The original poster of 1856 for the Parracombe Cattle Fair, subsequently held every August.

John Blackmore rebuilt the house in 1791 (the same year that East Bodley was refurbished). It was twice destroyed by fire before Charles Blackmore restored it and substituted its thatch for slate.

White's directory of 1878 offers a few more snippets on life in Victorian Parracombe. A cattle fair apparently dating back to 1856 was held annually in August with as many as 500 sheep and 100 oxen offered for sale. We are told that in the 1870s the Post Office was in the hands of R C Davey, that letters came via Barnstaple and that the nearest money order and telegraph office could be found at Lynton.

The Ark (above St Petrock's Church and the modern-day A39) was originally a farm labourer's cottage built by Noah Palmer. Inevitably, locals dubbed it 'Noah's Ark'.

The 1881 Census of Barnstaple Union Workhouse reveals that two of the 189 residents originated from Parracombe. They were 67-year-old Philip Abbott, a farm labourer and twelve year old Robert Pole, listed as a scholar. It is likely but not certain that Abbott was a destitute widower while Pole was surely an orphan.

They were not the only Parracombe people to end up in Barnstaple at this time. Reuben Blackmore, of Court Place, was an apprentice draper at Daw's in Barnstaple for a spell of four years and four months. He returned to the village only for holidays.

In 1893 the Fox and Goose was demolished to make way for a modern hotel. Opposite was the building known as the town hall, used for rifle shooting among other activities. Village youngsters would occasionally earn pin money by fastening the skids of the brewery carts - operated by Crocombe & Sons - at the top of the hills and fetching water for the horses. It was a hazardous occupation as the following newspaper report reveals. 'A serious accident happened to Master Fred Smyth of Rock Cottage on Wednesday last week. Being at the top of the hill as a carriage came along he courteously lowered the drag. Ere it was in place the horse moved, the result being that the boy's thumb was caught between the wheel and the drag, smashing the top of it. Mr Court bound up the wounded member until the arrival of Dr Henley, under whose care the boy is progressing as well as could be expected.' (Fred was the eldest son of Arthur Smyth)

The Family & Commercial Hotel in its heyday. An interesting advert on the side of the barn is for 'North British Clincher Tyres'

Smuggler's Tales

The hotel was built in the same year the village mourned one of its most colourful characters, Richard Jones, a labourer, reveller and suspected smuggler, who died on Wednesday, 22nd February, probably aged more than 100. The Journal reported his funeral as follows.

'The deceased, who possessed a pewter plate with his initials and 1790 engraved on it, considered that as the date of his birth but the register of Trentishoe parish records his baptism as 1796. The coffin was carried by hand to Trentishoe Church, a distance of over three miles, and on ascending the hill to the church there were not less than a hundred persons in the procession. A boy of 10 when this century dawned, the deceased might have told some interesting reminisences, but living all his days in this obscure corner, he does not seem to have heard of the doings of the rest of the world, and beyond a few smuggling adventures he could no other tale unfold.' The Rev R W Oldham officiated at the funeral, the largest ever known at Trentishoe.

Another obituary tells how Jones worked as an agricultural labourer for John Crang of Walnor. 'Of a jovial disposition, he spent his money freely and few were the village revels that did not see the long wiry form of Dick Jones.' The report reveals that he never married, saved no money and was for some years in receipt of parish pay. He was apparently well cared for by his nephew Charles Gill.

The obituary continues: 'Nearly forty years ago, on the establishment of Parracombe Fair, the deceased had an adventure. It is the old custom before a fair can be started to parade the neighbourhood and read a proclamation announcing the event, and as the large farmers dispense a jug or two of beer a crowd generally accompanies. Dick Jones, as usual, ready for a frolic, although then over three score years of age, joined the procession and all went well until the arrival at one farm. For some reason the occupier took offence and ordered them off; a few loitered in the hope of beer, when the farmer emerged with this gun and fired. Dick Jones was the only one injured, some thirty shots being afterwards extracted. Dick was rather proud of this exploit.'

Clearly, the Jones family was made of stern stuff. Dick's mother Agnes died in 1841 at the age of 89 while his father Humphrey died in 1854, aged 92. Dick's sisters lived until the ages of 94 and 91.

One aspect of village life that goes unrecorded in directories or by Arthur Smyth is the number of people who emigrated from Parracombe during the 19th and early 20th centuries. Thanks to research by David Blackmore we know that brothers Richard and William Blackmore both headed for America and settled in Newstead, New York. Richard (1792-1880) left first, probably before 1832, and was joined by his wife Philippa who crossed the Atlantic on the 'Calypso' in April 1833, sailing from Bideford. William (1796-1883) travelled on the Daedalus in about 1849. He was quickly joined by wife Charity, four of their children, an illegitimate grandchild as well as Charity's unmarried sister and her son.

Before long, a host of their nieces and nephews made the journey from Parracombe. Also among those who emigrated were John Lock Roach and his wife Ann (nee Lock) in 1848, William Lovering (born 1818), Charles Gammin (born 1821 in Trentishoe), who all headed for America. James Lord was one of five brothers from Trentishoe to emigrated to Australia in the 1850s. He returned to Parracombe in about 1890 to marry his second wife, the daughter of Richard Jones of Laurel House, before returning to Australia where he died in 1898 aged 67. There's evidence of more people leaving Parracombe in Chapter 10: Parracombe at War.

The 19th century was also the end of an era for the lime kiln standing at Heddon's Mouth. For an unknown number of decades limestone from South Wales was shipped here, to be burnt and spread on local fields to 'sweeten' the soil. The lime was also used in mortar and lime washes on buildings. However, it became cheaper to crush limestone rather than burn it and thus the kiln was abandoned before the 20th century. Its owners, the National Trust, have however, restored it several times in recent years.

A few remaining bottles and part of the top of a barrel from Crocombe's Brewery in Parracombe.

3 Character References

'A village is certainly no place for keeping things dark, If your business is such that you don't want other people to mind it, you'd best stay in town. But in a true village, in Parracombe, one child's prank is everybody's fun and one man's trouble is everybody's chance to help.'

The 1912 sales poster on which someone had recorded the sums paid at the auction. The Mill went for £305.

Blackmoor Gate sheep market illustrating the number of people who had a direct interest in market prices.

As the 20th century dawned Parracombe was a thriving country community. In 1902 Kelly's Trades Directory has both Richard Bowden and John Tamlyn as Parracombe wheelwrights, G. Court & Sons as village auctioneers and Crocombe & Sons as brewers. Andrew Delbridge is listed as the shoe maker, Daniel Gould as shopkeeper and Martha Hawkes as a grocer. Richard Rottenbury & Sons appear as blacksmiths, George Sommerwill as a mason and historian Arthur Smyth, of Rock Cottage, is the local agent for the Hand-in-Hand Insurance Company. By now the Fox & Goose had a landlady in charge - Miss Mary Sadler although it was owned by George Court. Before his death in 1905 George Court sold the pub to Henry Blackmore who had previously run taverns in London. Blackmore became well known as the publican although his tenure was not without problems. He was kicked by a horse - newspaper reports outline three diffent sets of circumstances for the accident. What is certain is that his leg was amputated six weeks later.

Thanks to the memories of a later George Court in 2003, and a 1921 edition of Kelly's, we begin to get a much more extensive picture of life in Parracombe during the 1920s and the activities of its 330-strong population. There were a wide range of trades and professions which in turn produced a remarkable degree of self sufficiency.

The cobbler was John de Lancey of Rose Cottage. The blacksmith, William Creek, had his workshop next to Holwell Farm and employed one assistant. The carpenter and undertaker was Mr Tamlyn, who lived in a cottage (since demolished) next to South Hill, alongside the sawpit at Pencombe. At the Fox & Goose the proprietors were now Mr and Mrs Fred Latham while the butcher was John de Lancey of Laburnum Cottage. Mr de Lancey worked from home and slaughtered animals in his back room. Meanwhile down at Mill House there was a general store run by Mrs Mary Antell, whose husband operated a horse and cart taxi service into Barnstaple twice a week. A sweet shop run by Mrs Hawkes at Dunbar Cottage was later re-located to Church Cottage in Churchtown.

The Brewery run by 'Maltster' Crocombe was in Malt House, Tarr Path (which was then known as Slippers Lane). Ern Smyth earned a living grinding grain at The Mill, which had been bought by Mr Crocombe in 1912. Two men, George Blackmore and Dick Crocombe, delivered the beer by horse and cart.

Mr Court's father was an auctioneer and merchant at London House, who had come to Parracombe from Exford in about 1865 to take over the veterinary business from his cousin, Mr Gooding. He also had an office in Barnstaple over the Midland Bank where he employed J C Webber and his sister Lily. Webber went on to found an estate agency that still thrives in North Devon today. The Courts held monthly markets at Blackmoor Gate, West Down, Mortehoe Station and West Buckland. They conducted the first pony auction at Cheriton which later evolved into the Brendon Pony Sale.

Two Miss Crocombes ran the Post Office (at its present location) where five postmen were employed. The mail arrived by train and Fred Antell used a hand cart to push it to the post office where it was sorted. He then set off by pony for Martinhoe and Woody Bay to do his round. At Woody Bay he waited in the postman's hut, just below The Trees, until it was time for the post box to be cleared. He then went back to Parracombe via Hunters Inn and Kittitoe where he emptied more post boxes. At 7pm he pushed his handcart containing outgoing mail back up to the Halt to catch the last train.

At the Old Post Office Arthur Parkhouse, the carpenter and undertaker, employed three men. Opposite, in the police station at Peel House, Sergeant Wilfred Hammacott and a constable would begin their daily beats on foot or by bike. There was no telephone at the police station, so messages were taken by Mr Court at London House.

Mr Delbridge operated a horse-and-carriage hire business from his home, Bardel, while his wife Mabel was a midwife. Before her marriage in 1924 Mabel lodged at the Old Post Office. Mr. Delbridge also worked at the quarry. Mrs Tossell ran a laundry from

To close the Trust Estate of Daniel Gould deceased.

PARRACOMBE, NORTH DEVON.

HIGHLY IMPORTANT SALE

OF

DWELLING HOUSES,

COTTAGES, GRIST MILLS,

Mineral Water Factory, Premises, Stables, Stores,

AND

ACCOMMODATION LANDS.

Herbert W. Court

Has been favoured with instructions to Sell by Public Auction, at the TOWN HALL, PARRACOMBE,

On THURSDAY, AUGUST 15th, 1912,

At 3 o'clock in the afternoon, (under the Conditions of the Devon and Exeter Law Association, and special Conditions to be then read) the following or in such other Lots as may then be decided.

Lot 1.—An Accommodation Field of rich Meadow or Pasture, known as Crosspark, No. 456 on the Ordnance Map, and containing thereby 2a. 1r. 3p. now in the occupation of Mr. John Barrow. Rent £9.
This field is admirably adapted for Small Holdings and for building purposes. It lies high, faces South, and adjoins the Main Road from Parracombe to Lynton.

Lot 2.—A Substantially Built Dwelling House and Premises, with Cartway, occupied by Mr. E. C. Wood, situate in the Village of Parracombe, opposite the Post Office. The House contains 5 Rooms and Outdoor Stores, and there is a good Well of Water. Rent £5.

Lot 3.—A Cottage and Garden, occupied by Miss A Dovell, adjoining Lot 2, and containing 4 Rooms, with use of Cartway, Well, and Pump on Lot 2. Rent £2/10s.

Lot 4.—A Cottage (nearly adjoining Lot 3,) with Woodhouse, with use of Cartway, W.C., Drying Ground, Pump and Well adjoining Lot 2, occupied by Mr. W. T. Tossell, containing 4 Rooms. Rent £4.

Lot 5.—A Dwelling House and Garden, occupied by Mr. George Antell, and situate in the Village of Parracombe, containing 6 Rooms and Outhouses. Rent £5.

Lot 6.—A Dwelling House, Stables, Coach house, Stores, and Garden adjoining Lot 5, occupied by Mr. E. Smyth. The House contains 6 Rooms. The whole would be very suitable for Business Premises. Rent £7.

Lot 7.—A Dwelling House, Garden and Shed, occupied by Miss E. Smyth. This House is very substantially built, and contains 7 Rooms and Offices. It stands in the centre of the Village and is very suitable either for Private Residence or for Business purposes. Rent £12.

Lot 8—A large Cart Shed, now in hand, adjoining Lot 7, in Vendor's possession.

Lot 9.—A Cart Shed or Store, close to the Fox and Goose Hotel occupied by Mr. G. Antell.

Lot 10.—Accommodation Land, being part of Bridge Meadow, Containing about half an acre, with two Linhays, now in the occupation of Mr. F. Smyth. This Lot adjoins Lot 9, and the River Heddon. It is an excellent piece of Building or Accommodation Land, near the centre of the Village.

Lot 11—Stable with loft over, Dung-pit and right of Cartway thereto through Lot 12, situate in the Village, and now in the occupation of Mr. R. S. Allison.

Lot 12—Parracombe Mills, including a Dwelling House (containing 8 Rooms), and Garden, now in the occupation of Mr. Thomas Skinner, Grist Mills and Sheds, with the Mill Pond and Rights of Water, in the occupation of Mr. F. R. Crocombe, and used as a Mineral Water Factory and Grist Mills. Also Stables and Yards, in the occupation of Mr. F. J. Court. Total Rent, £33/2s.
All the three parts together form one compact Set of Premises and should be eagerly sought after by persons desirous of opening any Business in Parracombe and requiring Water Power.

Tenants pay the outgoings.

Possession of the various Lots can be had either at Michaelmas or at Lady-day next.

The Auctioneer has very great pleasure in calling the attention of the Public generally to this important announcement, as the whole is intended for absolute Sale, to close a Trust Estate

To view apply to the Tenants, and for further particulars to the Auctioneer at Parracombe, or to

MR. LOUIS LOVIBOND,

Solicitor, BRIDGWATER & BURNHAM, SOMERSET.

Parracombe, 8th July, 1912.

POOLE'S West of England Steam Printing Works, ...lton.

her house next to the RAOB hall. The field alongside became known as the Drying Field until the hall was built. Sick villagers were tended by the district nurse, Mrs Antell, who carried out all calls by bicycle from her home The Nook.

The school attendance officer, Mr Davis, lived at Orchardside. As well as Parracombe, he was in charge of Martinhoe, Barbrook, Lynton, Lynmouth, Countisbury and Brendon schools, and must have been a familiar - if not always welcome - sight on his bike.

Two bakers from Combe Martin and one from Lynmouth called in at the village, travelling by horse and cart, while butchers from both Lynton and Combe Martin included Parracombe on their rounds. Hardware, haberdashery and groceries were delivered by cart from Combe Martin and a grocer brought in vegetables from Lynton. Two tailors, Mr Daw and Mr Gillard, were regular visitors from Barnstaple courtesy of the Lynton & Barnstaple Railway. Coal merchants operated from Moorlands, presumably because the train dropped off bulk supplies at Woody Bay Station.

It was in this era that a road to bypass the village was constructed. Devon County Council welcomed the project as a way of finding work for men left jobless following the closure of local factories and a shipyard. At a meeting in 1923 it was described as 'ideal for the absorption of unskilled labour'. Although six tons of dynamite were brought in from elsewhere the rest of the material needed was found locally and the quarry enjoyed something of a heyday. The road's cost was estimated at £27,000.

In the 1930 edition of Kelly's the Rev John Chanter is described as 'lord of the manor' and Heddon Hall is still known as The Rectory. Fred Latham remains at the Fox & Goose and Arthur Parkhouse continues as local carpenter (although by now he's doubling up as sub-postmaster). Arthur Smyth has moved to the butcher's place - Laburnum Cottage. By 1930 there is the first clear sign locally of farming's increasing mechanisation following the establishment of the Anglo-American Oil Company's fuel depot at Blackmoor Gate.

Five years later Kelly's has William Creek at the Fox & Goose, Maude Kingdom as the district nurse, living at Hills View (now Renaissance House) and Miss Florence Smyth running a Friendly Society from Bridge House, prior to her marriage to Arthur Parkhouse.

The Royal Antediluvian Order of Buffaloes had branches or 'lodges' across the UK. It was a fund-raising, fraternal organisation, financially responsible for numerous good causes. According to a booklet written in 1940 by Bro W Blackmore about its history, the Lodge was opened in December 1925 and the founders were Primos Gye, Sutton, Tucker and Widden. The booklet says there were sixteen initiations in the first year and only 39 were recorded before the outbreak of the Second World War, when average attendance numbered 11.

When it started the Lodge had no home to call its own so, in 1927, a building fund was started. Driving force behind the building project was Bro 'Tommy' Barson who organised draws, competitions, concerts, whist drives and dances to generate funds. Bro Blackmore acknowledges: ' . . . every Brother worked hard and made every sacrifice and the credit is due to the Lodge as a whole but, at the same time Bro Barson is the one who made the Hall possible and his name will live in the History of the Lodge as the one mainly responsible for our great efforts which are by no means finished.'

In 1931 the Heddon Valley Lodge was given the hall site by Mrs Jackson, wife of the late Reverend Jackson (himself a Buff), on the condition it was built upon within two years. Lodge records show that she paid £2 4s for the transfer of deeds.

In May 1932 Bro Arthur Parkhouse put in the successful £740 tender for building the hall. The brothers dug the foundations themselves and clearly took great pride in their new meeting place. A Foundation Stone Laying Ceremony took place in June that year, with stones being laid by Bro Fry

(Provincial Grand Primo), Bro Barson, Mrs Jackson and Mrs Henningsen, 'a generous supporter', among others. At the time of its official opening in October Bro Barson had loaned the building fund £150. The following year a mortgage of £400 at four per cent was negotiated with the Misses Dovell (sisters of Mrs Jackson) so the final bills could be paid. In 1939 we learn that Primo P Tucker presented a 'magnificent pair of buffalo horns' to the Lodge (they remain on show).

At first the building was inadequately lit by a handful of Tilley lamps and although two more of these were acquired in 1934 it must have been a gloomy, shadowy place in winter. Neither was it terribly warm. By 1935 the Brothers decided to have a heating system installed by a Barnstaple workman at a cost of £65.

Nine years later the lighting was improved by Calor gas lamps, bought at a cost of £28 10s and paid for by Brother Barson. The price was reduced by £5 as the contractor, J Moore of South Molton, took the now-redundant Tilley lamps as trade-ins.

Medicinal whisky

At this time it cost 24s to hire the hall for an evening or £2 10s for the day. It was often used for whist drives, dances and even children's exercise classes. One commercial user was Mr Knight of Barnstaple, whose Mobile Cinematograph Company provided regular film shows.

Despite the pressures of building costs Buffs in Parracombe helped finance Dorothy Tremllet and her brother in the Orders' Orphanage. When she returned to her home in South Molton in August 1940 Brother Williams reported that 'by her manner and how she was dressed and her education would enable her to take her place in any business house in the country as a typist.' Sadly, her mother did not wish her to follow a profession 'therefore all efforts of the Order have been wasted on this girl'.

Throughout the 1930s Brother Polkinghorne appeared on the Alms List. He was apparently frail and elderly and his mental health was deteriorating. He was frequently sent gifts of 5s or 10s and sometimes requested help with bills. The Brothers tried to win him an annuity from the Order, and, having investigated his personal finances, made several submissions, all of which failed.

On admission to the Cottage Hospital in Lynton he was visited regularly by a Brother who supplied his whisky. The daily glass (prescribed by the nurse) was soon raised to three a day by the doctor but this agreeable state of affairs couldn't continue forever. Eventually Brother Polkinghorne had to be moved to the Poor Law Institute in Barnstaple. His wife was distressed about the possible costs of his funeral so the Buffs agreed to meet his bills.

The Brothers continued to visit Polkinghorne in Barnstaple and sent him raffle prizes, mostly cigarettes. When they discovered that his wife survived on just 5s a week, they gave her money as well. Finally, in fulfilment of their promise, the Buffs paid for his funeral at Christchurch. According to Bro Blackmore, more than £50 was paid out in Benevolent Fund Grants in 17 years.

Audrey Petherick, born at East Bodley Farm in 1923, has some fond memories of childhood in Parracombe.

'I used to see Uncle Ern (Ernest Smyth) turning the heap of barley which was on the floor of the Malt House in Slipper's Lane. I think the barley was allowed to sprout, then used to brew the beer.

'I remember my father saying that they used to take a jug down to the brewery to collect some "barm". This was the froth that formed on the surface of the fermenting beer. It was used to make barm cake, a sort of yeasty cake.

'We had great excitement one Sunday evening when a rat got in the back kitchen. Rover, the old dog, enjoyed a good rat hunt. He chased it round the kitchen until the rat hid under a facket of wood in the corner. Rover flushed it out and chased it into the passage, nearly upsetting the drain pipe of walking sticks, and into the front kitchen.

'The rat dived into the front of the organ and Rover, in full cry, jumped onto the organ pedals but couldn't get at it. We pulled the organ away from the wall, Rover tore a hole in the back canvas and out bolted the rat. It belted across the kitchen, found a gap in the top passage door, leapt up over the glass case with the stuffed heron in, scrambled over great aunt Bessie's jars of jam on the top shelf and disappeared through a small hole in the wall, free at last, leaving a disappointed Rover and some smashed jars of jam.'

Dave and Nettie Rawle moved to Holworthy Farm in 1948, struggling to pay the £3,600 it cost them. The farmhouse was not only troubled by rats feasting in an upstairs granary but also by a cockroach colony which lived behind the fireplace. The insects were everywhere and would crawl into the pockets of coats hanging on a chair or burrow themselves into laundry. Nettie solved the crisis after receiving some sound advice from her mother.

'My mum, who lived at Withypool, sent us a letter that she had cut out of the paper about how to get rid of cockroaches,' she recalls. 'In every infestation of cockroaches there is a queen, like in a swarm of bees, and she is white.

'One night I was sitting by the fire and I saw her. Anyway, I stalked away and got a jam pot. It came out a bit further and I put the jam pot on it and then got a bit of paper to make sure it was in the jam pot. We hadn't got a sink so I took my jam pot outside and took my kettle and poured boiling water over it, to make sure it was dead.

'And do you know, within the next day there were beetles *[cockroaches]* dead on the floor and, within a week, you couldn't go in as the floor was black with beetles. You could sweep them up by the bucketful and they went from large to the size of a flea. And we've never had a black beetle since.'

Dr Ernest Mold remembers setting up a surgery at Parracombe in 1953, the year he started working in Lynton. At first it took place at Gwennie Crocker's house, across the road from the chapel. Soon afterwards the Crockers moved and Dr Mold moved his surgery to 'The Rectory' in Bodley Lane, now known as Pimbury. With a change of Rector came another switch in venue for the doctor, this time to Robin's Nest, the home of the Weatherall-Kings. He practiced there at least until the arrival of Dr Roger Ferrar in 1970. By then a health centre had been built in Lynton and transport links between Parracombe and its neighbouring town had improved substantially. Subsequently, Parracombe's surgery was closed.

When Dr Mold first began work at the Crockers they had just installed a bathroom. Soon afterwards, the road was dug up three times in short order - first by the newly-created water board to lay a mains supply, then by the electricity board and, finally, for the installation of sewage pipes.

'I used to enjoy talking to the old inhabitants,' recalled Dr Mold. 'Mr Creek who ran the Fox & Goose, Mr Butts at his sweet shop at London House, Mr Parkhouse, the undertaker and his wife, once the postmistress at the Old Post Office, Mr Latham at Dale View, the two Miss Blackmores, Mr and Mrs Hagley at Paradise View . . . and many more. I was in close touch with the Police Station, of course, but I often thought that the lone policemen there must have felt a bit cut off.'

No B***** swearing

On 3rd July 1954 the national *Picture Post* featured Parracombe in a celebration of village life. Bill Hagley was recorded as a road-mender, grave-digger, bell-ringer and drum-player in the village band. Bill Creek, publican at the Fox & Goose, explained why swearing was banned. 'Any lady can come into my bar, at any time, and play skittles or darts without hearing anything unfit', he pronounced. The accordion-playing rector, John Lynn, visited daily for a single drink and, as Mr Creek gleefully informed the *Post*: 'If the parson had another, all the village would know by morning'.

At the school the article focused on an infant class

Parracombe Band. Obviously not only accomplished musicians but early exponents of the traffic cone (it is not known whether any royalties for the adoption of this invention are due to Parracombe Revels).

compiling a daily newspaper. Stories included snippets such as 'the farmers are beginning to sow the corn,' or 'Michael's granny's geese are trying to run away' or 'Tony's father has a new tractor. It is a 44 horse-power diesel'.

Then sheep farmer Reg Dallyn offered a little homespun wisdom to the *Post* journalist: 'Townsfolk wonder what we do with ourselves out here,' he said. 'Well, what with being leader of the Blackmoor Gate Young Farmers' Club, giving shearing classes, being Chairman of the Rifle Club, a member of the Hall Committee up at Martinhoe and singing in the choir - I'm as busy as a pup with its first flea.'

The feature ended with the following observation: 'A village is certainly no place for keeping things dark, If your business is such that you don't want other people to mind it, you'd best stay in town. But in a true village, in Parracombe, one child's prank is everybody's fun and one man's trouble is everybody's chance to help.'

The article appeared in the same year that Parracombe was finally connected to mains electricity. This momentous event happened more than half a century after street lighting was installed in Lynton, where the town's benefactor George Newnes had provided a state-of-the-art hydro-electric plant. (It was, however, washed away by the Lynmouth flood of 1952.)

Lower down the Heddon Valley electricity arrived later still. On 2nd May 1958 the North Devon Journal

In 1967 Jeremy Thorpe, then MP for North Devon, attends the formal opening of the the playing field by Mrs Hutchinson, niece of Robert St John Allison who donated the field in 1937.

reported that TV presenter Cliff Michelmore and his wife Jean Metcalfe, a presenter on radio's popular 'Two Way Family Favourites', delayed returning from a holiday at Hunter's Inn so that they could 'officially' flick the switch that would light up the valley. The supply went to five farms, one hotel and 17 other properties.

The playing field was given to the parish by Mr. Paddy Allison before the start of the Second World War, although it wasn't until 1967 that it was level and usable. Villagers had been raising money for the project since 1952 and proceeds from Parracombe Revels helped towards the £925 cost of preparation work. The official opening of the field coincided with the 1967 Revels and Alice Hutchinson, a niece of Mr Allison, performed the ceremony.

North Devon MP Jeremy Thorpe planted a flowering cherry tree on behalf of those who had helped raise funds for the project and suggested the field should take the name of Sir Francis Chichester, whose family home was Shirwell Rectory and who that year had become first to sail single-handedly around the world. In fact it remained the Coronation playing field, for King George VI's coronation on 12th May 1937.

The Womens' Institute has long been a pillar of rural life and in 1961 Parracombe had an active local branch. The president that year was Mrs Parrish, her deputies were Mrs Nicholls and Miss Matthews and the secretary was Mrs Paul. At monthly meetings there was a talk or demonstration and also a competition. In January 1961 the challenge was to prepare a 'packed workman's lunch (sic) costing two shillings and six pence'. In March there was a prize for the best home made hat while in November members were asked to depict themselves when they were young.

In 1967 the 13 ft wheel at the Mill House turned again after a restoration project carried out by Peter Teal. In an article for the 1968 Exmoor Review he described how the mechanism of the mill had been abandoned after the last miller joined the army in 1942. Despite this Mr Teal, a spinning wheel maker, decided to buy the property from a list of 14 old mills he'd researched across southwest England.

'I thought Parracombe Mill the most attractive, had the greatest possibilities, and it was in an area where property values are very low,' he wrote. 'It only cost £1,000.'

He found the wheel - 3.9 metres (13 ft) in diameter and 1 metre (three ft) wide - largely intact although half-buried in mud. It took nine months to free it, a process that involved demolishing a barn and removing cover stones from a culvert. Finally, by autumn 1963, the wheel pit and tail race were cleared of all accumulated silt, rubbish and rusting machinery.

That was just the start. In a labour of love, Mr Teal had to saw off 252 rusty bolts and painstakingly punch the threads out of the cast iron wheel rim. In February 1966 he ordered 1.5 tons of new elm worth £35 from the Knightshayes Estate at Tiverton and spent much of the summer fashioning it into a new wheel. On 24th June 1967 Jeremy Thorpe - presumably fresh from his duties up on the Coronation Field - cut a ribbon to send water cascading down the wheel's 42 wooden buckets.

It's worth noting that this project was much more than one man's idle fancy. The wheel generated electricity, which Mr Teal used both for drying timber and to power the lathes on which his spinning wheels were made.

The Seventies was dominated by a debate on absentee landlords, the effect this had on the village shops, problems with drought and the reluctance of South West Water to provide a pipeline from Blackmoor Gate. Another hot topic was the unprepossessing appearance of the overhead wires which criss-cross the heart of the village even today.

During the 1980s TV reception in Parracombe was patchy and sometimes non-existent. In 1984 residents formed the Parracombe Community Television Association with Tim Cotter-Stone from the Fox & Goose as chair. A combination of various grants and the proceeds of a local '200 club' raised enough money to erect a village 'transposer' aerial in 1986. Eighteen years later it is still in business, picking up four of the five analogue national television channels from Caradon Hill, 50 miles north of Plymouth, and re-transmitting them at low power on different frequencies to about 50 houses in and around the village.

The mast is sited in the field above 'Bardell' with a small wooden box housing the electronics. After the height of the aerial was restricted by Exmoor National Parks and the power of the transmitters by the broadcasting authorities, it became clear that homes beyond Prisonford could not be served by the aerial. Those residents who did benefit - mainly at Pencombe Rocks, Bodley Lane and East Hill - formed the Parracombe Community Television Association and (after a few initial problems with subscriptions) contributed to the £500 annual cost of maintaining the aerial.

Unfortunately, it wasn't the end of reception difficulties. Television pictures were still subject to interference from the likes of high pressure weather systems, rising tree sap, power cuts and a host of other intractable problems. The most serious setback occurred on 25th January 1990 when the mast was brought down by a gale. A new, stronger version was installed soon afterwards (secured by three guy ropes) and a renewal of the electronics in 2000 greatly improved performance.

In the early 1990s there was outrage among villagers when South West Water insisted that Parracombe's water supply would in future be piped from Bratton Fleming rather than the village's underground spring, which had its own mini-treatment plant. The spring had failed only once in recent times - the dry summer of 1989 - but following a downpour SWW tested the water and concluded it contained potentially harmful bugs. Vocal support from some farmers who feared water shortages was drowned out by fierce opposition.

Villagers mounted a campaign against the SWW plans, stories appeared in the national press and local MP Nick Harvey described the company's £300,000 proposal as 'a project that no one wants or apparently needs'. It was all to no avail. SWW ultimately got its way although it did donate an inscribed stone trough - nicknamed 'The Coffin' by locals - which was set outside St Petrock's church as a memorial to the old supply. The trough collects spring water from the moors for anyone still brave enough to take a sip!

To mark the millennium a giant piece of slate echoing the ancient longstone was put up at Parracombe Lane Head, where the road through the village meets the A39 to Lynton. Beneath lies a time capsule filled by villagers and schoolchildren.

One hundred years previously the village was commercially robust. But at the start of the 21st century Parracombe was reduced to one post office/shop and a single pub. The jobs of wheelwright, blacksmith, dressmaker, butcher and cobbler were a long distant memory. Although the shops at Lynton and Combe Martin are closer most villagers depend on Barnstaple for shopping and plenty of villagers work there too. At least a regular and dependable bus service ensures shoppers or workers without a car can reach their destination.

Miss J Fitzsimmons taking the part of Lady Horfield, with Mary Court and Carol Nicholls playing the parts of her daughters in 'Treasure from France' - a WI production. Probably staged in the late 1950s.

4 Life on the Land

Farming has always been the primary business of Parracombe although historically there were plenty of associated trades operating in the village. When yields were plentiful villagers were relatively well-heeled. If the weather was inclement or crops were poor people had to tighten their belts.

Blackmoor Gate Market refreshment rooms in the late 1920s.

In this chapter we've concentrated on farming at Heale, not least because there are some good written and first-hand sources covering the past century. However the agricultural picture would have been very similar in Parracombe and indeed the whole of rural North Devon. Above all, this was a time of huge upheaval - driven by mechanisation and new technology.

Heale lies in a sheltered combe just over 2 miles northwest of Parracombe. Walking towards the sea along what is now a dead-end road, there are some marvellous views from the top of the hill as you descend into the hamlet. Above the rooftops stand the heather-clad coastal hills of Trentishoe and, looking beyond, the Bristol Channel and the Welsh coast.

During research for this book we came across a treasure-trove of farming records in the form of a set of accounts, believed to relate to a Heale farm between 1895 and 1926. They are interspersed with notes on planting, tilling, varieties of crops and general husbandry but they are incomplete, frequently altered and don't always make clear which items relate to income and which to expenditure. They become increasingly sketchy towards the end of the period. Here are some selected abstracts:

Income from 25th March 1899			**£**	**s**	**d**
May	4	Mrs Sloley	11	7	0
	12	Jas Tucker Lamb	1		
		Ditto 3 bags potatoes@ 4s		12	0
June	9	Jas Tucker Lamb 34lb@ 9d per lb	1	5	6
	16	Jas Tucker Lamb 32 lbs @ 9d per lb	1	4	0
	23	Jas Tucker Lamb 33lbs @ 9d per ;b	1	4	9
July	4	Jas Tucker Lamb 34 lbs @ 9d per lb	1	5	6
Sept	11	Jas Tucker 2 Lambs @ 8d per lb	2	4	0
	14	Jas Tucker 12 Lambs @ 13s 6d each	8	2	0
	18	Mrs Sloley bought cow + calf Tulip commission 2s 3d	14	10	0
Oct	2	Mr Smith Westlandpound 6 ewes .9s 0d each commission 3s 0d	8	11	9
	16	Sold Lottie Mr Johns Blackmoor Auction	11	19	6
Nov	3	Jas Tucker for grass keep at Middleton	5	0	0
Oct	27	Jas Pile part of pig at 7s 6d per score	3	16	0
1900					
Jan	6	Mr Sloley keep for Bullocks + dog	14	12	0
Jan	13	Foresters Club 5 weeks 3 days	3	6	0
Feb	7	Mr T Isaac Cow +calf (Cherry)	13	17	6
	27	Messrs Flow + Co 20 bags of potatoes @ 3s 6d per bag	3	10	0
May	3	Mr Isaac 2 stear yearlings	14	0	0
		Mr Jones 32 bsh oats @ 2s 4d per bsh	3	14	8
	5	Mrs Tucker Part of pig 9s per score	2	8	0
		Sold Lyntons 6 bags of potatoes @ 5s	1	10	0
		Mrs Sloley	9	0	0
			128	0	2

So in this *period, just over a year, the farm income can be broken down as follows:*

Sale of lamb by the pound *(presumably butcher meat)*	£17 5s 9d
Sale of pig meat	£7 4s 0d
Sale of Livestock	£62 18s 9d
Sale of Potatoes	£5 0s 0d
Sale of Oats	£3 14s 8d
Keep of Animals	14 12 0d
Grass Keep	£5 0s 0d
Club Payment	£3 6s 10d
Mrs Sloley *(probably butter - inference from other years)*	£20 6s 0d

Expenditure itemised for the same period amounts to £160 8s 3½d. Apart from feed bills, and a number of unspecified invoices, other purchases include 2 pigs, 3 ewe lambs, butter scales, coal, rent for grass at Middleton and wages for Albert Smyth, who was paid £10 10s per year.

Most of the recorded income from this year comes from mixed farming. The farm may have done its own butchering and almost certainly made its own butter. However, unless it was running up massive debts it seems likely that other earnings for the year have not been fully recorded.

There is evidence throughout the notes of a much greater income potential, suggesting that farm diversification is anything but a modern idea! For example in 1898 there are income entries both for rabbits and a chicken. There are no entries for eggs but it is possible eggs and chickens were sold or perhaps used mainly at the family table. Income was also generated from stabling and haulage and we discover that in 1896 Mr Jones paid £100 rent for stables and £6 for grass keep for horses. The same year Messrs Crocombe and Sons (Parracombe) paid £1 4s 0d for horse labour and the Crocombe grass seed bill was £3 4s. A page of entries dating from 1895 amounts to £1 4s 3d and relates to the hauling of furniture, wood and coal. There's no indication as to whether this is money earned or spent.

Building new roads was and fencing the adjacent land was a hallmark of the 19th century.

12 inches = 1 foot
3 feet = 1 yard
5½ yards = 1 perch,
22 yards = 1 chain
10 chains = 1 furlong
8 furlongs = 1 mile

It's difficult to understand why such a simple measurement system was discarded in favour of decimalisation.

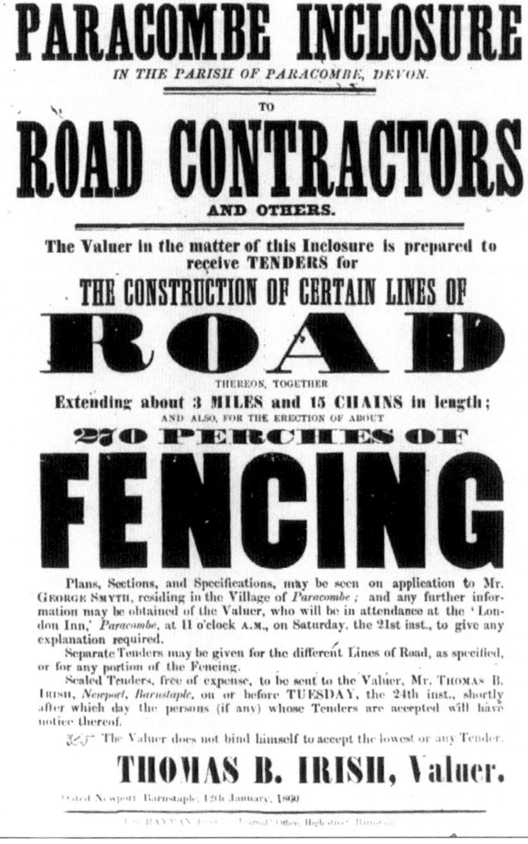

PARACOMBE INCLOSURE

IN THE PARISH OF PARACOMBE, DEVON.

TO

ROAD CONTRACTORS

AND OTHERS.

The Valuer in the matter of this Inclosure is prepared to receive TENDERS for

THE CONSTRUCTION OF CERTAIN LINES OF

ROAD

THEREON, TOGETHER

Extending about 3 MILES and 15 CHAINS in length;

AND ALSO, FOR THE ERECTION OF ABOUT

270 PERCHES OF

FENCING

Plans, Sections, and Specifications, may be seen on application to Mr. GEORGE SMYTH, residing in the Village of *Paracombe*; and any further information may be obtained of the Valuer, who will be in attendance at the 'London Inn,' *Paracombe*, at 11 o'clock A.M., on Saturday, the 21st inst., to give any explanation required.

Separate Tenders may be given for the different Lines of Road, as specified, or for any portion of the Fencing.

Sealed Tenders, free of expense, to be sent to the Valuer, Mr. THOMAS B. IRISH, *Newport, Barnstaple*, on or before TUESDAY, the 24th inst., shortly after which day the persons (if any) whose Tenders are accepted will have notice thereof.

The Valuer does not bind himself to accept the lowest or any Tender.

THOMAS B. IRISH, Valuer.

Dated Newport, Barnstaple, 12th January, [illegible]

In 1895 and 1896 substantial income was made from the rental of ground to over a dozen tenants, at anything from 7 yards to 38¾ yards per lease. In 1895 this produced income of £14 5s 6d and potato crop varieties included Holborn Abundance, Suttons Abundance and Daniels.

The general farm expenditure is less detailed. Many entries are just listings of bills paid to businesses with no record of the goods or services acquired. However in 1896 the accounts do show a payment to Mr Delbridge of 1s for heeling best boots and the settlement of accounts for barley meal, maize and flour. A new pair of boots was bought for 13s 6d and a payment of 5s 4d was made to the Foresters Club at Lynton (perhaps some kind of savings society or local insurance scheme similar to that operated by the Buffs in Parracombe).

In other years there appear payments for wages, farriers bills and, particularly, coal which in summer was 10s 6d for a ½ cwt but in winter cost 12s 6d for the same amount. In 1896 a manure sieve was bought for 2s and 24 yards of wire netting for 3s. Pigs and lambs were frequent purchases; a pig costing around 19s to £1 and lambs about 17s each.

By the start of the 20th century the entries become fewer and suggest the farmer is chasing income by whatever means available. There is a charge for labour to Mrs Tucker, a bill for trimming Mr Cruck's fences and a water course, sheep shearing charges to several farms and a sideline supplying wood. Other services involved cutting weeds, digging brambles, cleaning water pits and drains, and sowing grass for Fred Smythe.

Haulage was another important part of the business and orders included stone from Parracombe quarry, hauled slate, sand and lime and "4 loads of deads from front of Lower Shop" all for Mr J Bowden, earning £3 9s 3d. Rabbit sales did well and by 1903 earned more than £10. Meanwhile the farm garden helped balance the household budget through crops such as potatoes, onions, carrots, rhubarb, cabbages, runner beans, savoys, lettuce and strawberries.

Calving was spread throughout the year and we discover that Dorothy had a bull calf in November 1900, Fancy's calf came on 16th December and Daisy's on 26th February 1901. Lovely calved on 27th June 1901, Fairie on 5th August and Tulip on 4th October. Four years later Lovely, Fairie and Tulip were still calving and Cherry, Pink, Maggie, Beauty, Tiny and Topsy were also producing offspring. Dorothy had calved but produced no milk.

The principal crops were potatoes, oats, corn, barley, turnips, swedes and mangolds. The main

The dairy class outside East Bodley. On the left in the front row is Mrs Bessie Lock, who farmed East Bodley.

period for sowing oats was April with the harvest in August. Sowing of root crops went on through to mid-July and harvesting continued into January. Some field names are recorded and it's clear that grass, barley and oats were sown at Broadpiece in 1900, while Longlands had swedes, mangolds and 2 acres of oats. Outer Skirt was also planted with oats.

In 1909 South Park, New Mill, Home Park, Higher Marleycoombe, Outer Marlycoombe and Leapark are listed along with passing mentions of Square Close, Higher Barkham, Bangholme, Bidwell, the Piece, Loxhore Park, Water Field and Middle Field. However it is by no means certain that these were actually part of the farm.

Cost for labour and servants are recorded in varying detail. In 1897 Annie Garnish and Sydney Garnish were paid 1s a week and costs itemised under Annie's name suggest that in addition to her wage some personal items were provided, including 5d for a small tooth comb, 6d for aprons and bootlaces and 1s for lace.

Alice and Philip Latham were employed between 1907 and 1910 and Alice's expenditure is very closely itemised. She was paid 1s 3d per week and appears to have been well outfitted according to the sample below:

Pair black gloves			6½d
Hat and gloves		6s	5½d
2 pair busts			9d
Bon of paper			6d
5yrds of material for dress		9s	9½d
5yrds lining 6¾ pr yard		2s	10d
Making dress		3s	6d
trimming	£1	3s	0d
Belting silk and hook			3d
Bodice lining			7½d
Wages to Ladyday		16s	3d
3 yrds flanelette		1s	9d
2 yard of flanelette		1s	2d
Mending Bobb			6d
corsets		1s	19½d
For Hair D.....			6d
Bodices		1s	2d

Philip was paid 4s 4d per week but seems to have had less bought for him. 'Nail boots, best boots and socks for same, a cardigan jacket and 2 pair of stockings' were all that were listed in a 9 month period against his signature. Later payments to the Foresters Club are noted under Philip's name and he was bought breeches at 9s.

Payments for casual labour are recorded, such as on 23rd August 1895 when Mr Delve was paid 5s for corn harvest. It must have been thirsty work because squeezed into the rows below his entry is a payment for 4s 6d for 4½ gallons of beer from the Pugsleys!

The journal provides a wealth of detail on a complex business which is maximising every opportunity to make money. The core operation is a mixture of arable and livestock farming with a secondary income from stabling and, towards the end of the period, haulage. Although expenditure on the business and the servants is fairly clear it's difficult to be sure about the household accounts.

We can gain more evidence of life at Heale from

A quart milk bottle from the dairy at East Bodley.

Claude Rogers of Mill Farm ploughing with heavy horses circa 1950.

A corn harvest picnic at Newberrys in the late 1930s. On the cart: Freddie Smyth, Charles Smyth, Frederick Smyth and Archie Smyth. Seated: Kathleen Smyth, Jenny Smyth, Bessie Lock, Audrey Smyth, Ada Smyth (nee Crocombe) and Thomas Crocombe. Not forgetting Violet, an ex army horse .

the memories of Georgie Bray who was born at Walner Farm in 1903 and lived there for at least 30 years. Her recollections were audio-taped by the present owner, Phil Griffiths, when she returned at his invitation in 1992.

Many of Georgie's anecdotes concern a plague of rats around the farm and farmhouse, where they could be heard running behind walls and beneath floors. A cat lover, she awoke one night and lit a candle to see that her cat had proudly brought a dead rodent in through the window and deposited it on her bed. Rats also over-ran a storage barn and ruined the apples from four acres of orchards.

When Georgie's father realised the creatures were coming into the farmhouse near a bedroom, he decided it was time for a little rat-like cunning of his own. His daughter takes up the story:

'He went and got a rabbit, put some strychnine in it and tied it to the bannister. The next morning there was nothing left. He did the same again and the following morning there was nothing left. He got a third but they didn't touch much of that one. It was three weeks before we could go back into the bedroom for the smell of dead rats but we never got rats and mice again after that.'

It was just as well because the family depended on taking in guests to raise extra money. One young man staying at Walner to learn about farming became poorly after walking in severe weather to Blackmoor Gate to catch the Barnstaple train. A Lynton doctor was called and arrived by motorbike. He diagnosed diptheria and young Georgie was quickly charged with nursing the poor fellow back to health.

Diptheria, a bacterial infection of the throat, has largely been eliminated in the Western world now. At that time however it caused numerous deaths, particularly among children. Consequently, Georgie and her patient remained in isolation for weeks until he had recovered. 'I didn't see my family for a month,' she recalled. 'Everything that was brought to me was left outside the door. I did everything for him but I wouldn't wash his face. I thought I must not let him breathe on me.' This seems to have occurred while she was still at Parracombe school.

After his convalescence Georgie was urged to seek medical training by Parracombe's district nurse. In fact, she tired of helping the sick after yet more of Walner's visitors became ill and turned to her as resident nurse. She left school a month before her 14th birthday, intending to be a dressmaker, but her hopes of visiting Mrs Burden in Parracombe for dressmaking lessons were dashed when her brother insisted she help around the farm instead.

A year later she was sent to an uncle and his wife on a smallholding at Westbury, Wiltshire, where she earned a pittance. 'I used to have to do all the work cleaning inside the house and mixing the pig food and the cow food,' she remembered. 'It really broke my heart because (my aunt) was so very mean.'

It seems the miserly woman pilfered money sent by Georgie's mother although the uncle secretly left small amounts of cash in Georgie's bag, urging her not to mention it to his wife.

Two other uncles went to Australia. One left the ship at Darwin while the other stayed aboard, only be lost at sea when it foundered shortly afterwards. However the surviving brother returned to Walner much later, bringing a box of Australian fruit with him. Another uncle emigrated to New Zealand and as a young woman Georgie was invited to visit by her cousin. Sadly for her, her mother wouldn't let her go.

The Pethericks were another well-known Heale farming family and Robert John Petherick, born at home on 22nd May 1931, has contributed some fascinating detail to this book. He was barely six years old when he started at the village school and as there was no transport he usually had to walk the two-and-a-half mile route both ways.

Sometimes he hitched an early ride with an aunt bound for market at Lynton, her horse and trap loaded up with butter, chicken, cream and parsley. His only chance of a lift home though was when horses from his own or a neighbouring farm were at Parracombe's smithy for shoeing (this was a time when ploughs were all horse-drawn). Consequently John always looked in on the blacksmith as he headed home - just in case.

At the time crops grown at Heale included corn, swedes, turnips and flatpoles (cabbages). The farm was stocked with Devon cows and closewool sheep and about 40 turkeys were reared for Christmas. Like other farmers the Pethericks trapped rabbits and sold them to a wholesaler who collected the bodies by lorry and paid for them by the pound.

John's mother made butter and cream and it frequently fell to the children to deliver bucketloads to Hunters Inn during high season where there was brisk business to be had among coach trippers. Livestock was driven to Blackmoor Gate market and lambs struggling to complete the trip were often put on a cart. Even so, the journey could take more than three hours. Market days always included a square meal at the Blackmoor Gate Hotel, long since demolished. Once livestock markets were held at Woody Bay, on land above the station, and also Barbrook but business was so brisk at Blackmoor Gate that two auctioneers were fully employed.

Archie Smyth raking with the 'Huxtable Expanding Rake'. Holwell, circa 1950.

When the farm - one of three in the hamlet - was busy at harvest or shearing times John was allowed to stay at home and help out. At times like these the neighbours all mucked in and the hard physical labour was slightly eased by the sense of a social occasion. John eventually left school aged 14, just as the Second World War was in its closing stages. Farm labourers were by this time vital to the national interest as food shortages continued to bite hard.

John worked on the farm full time and remembers liming the ground as being a messy business. Lorries delivered the lime bags and the contents were spread from the back of a horse and cart. Afterwards the farm's three horses had to be carefully washed to remove all trace of the sticky lime residue.

After the war John was employed by a contractor and frequently put in charge of a threshing machine.

Rabbits for lunch? Ethel Petherick (right) with visitors from London at Higher Heale during the war

His working day was long but as there were no lights on farm vehicles it at least ended promptly at sundown. The journey home was always tortuous because the family tractor struggled to top eight miles per hour.

Socially, John went to the rifle club at Parracombe, the Young Farmers' Club, card parties (including whist drives at Moorlands Hotel and Martinhoe Hall) and various local dances. His mode of transport was invariably cycle or horseback.

After marrying in 1958 John rented a farm at Brendon, keeping cows, sheep and chickens, and didn't returned to full-time work at Heale until his father's retirement in 1967. In his early years he farmed 'half crease', which meant looking after a flock of sheep for someone else and keeping half the lambs it produced.

In 1997 John Petherick junior took over the farm, now amounting to 170 acres. Every year he makes around 30 acres of baled hay and 18 acres of silage. The rest is used for sheep and beef grazing. Lambs come from a Suffolk ram and a flock of Exmoor Horn and crossbreed ewes. Replacement ewes come from a Bluefaced Leicester ram and Exmoor Horn ewes.

Lambs are still sold at Blackmoor Gate but the days when John snr. paid the farm rent with his wool check are long gone. Today prices quoted by the Wool Marketing Board at South Molton are, comparatively, very low. John jnr. now keeps Charolais-cross cows - not Devons which became uneconomic in the 1970s as they bear fatter meat so must be kept for longer before slaughter. The house cow that provided John snr. with milk in the home is also a thing of the past.

The farm benefits from payments made under an Environmentally Sensitive Areas agreement although John is no longer allowed to stock Heale Moor. As a result, it is largely covered in gorse. There are other agricultural subsidies which weren't available to his father but this means a substantial amount of extra paperwork. Usually his wife, Janet, takes on this task. One traditional chore - the liming of fields - is still carried out but as it's costly, it isn't done so often.

Like his father John jnr supports the Young Farmers Club and appreciates the social outlet it offers the whole family. Years ago YFC members were farmers-in-waiting; these days many will never enjoy a career in agriculture. John's eldest daughter, Ann, is in the hotel trade although his two other children, Julie and Martin, may eventually work the land.

In the last 20 years Heale has flourished in terms of population, though not through any renaissance in farming. In 1982 there were four dwellings, two of which formed the centrepieces of substantial family farms - Higher Heale and Heale. These each came with 150 acres and a range of traditional buildings.

The other two dwellings were effectively smallholdings formed from Court Farm. The old cottage was extended and new farm buildings erected to establish Heale Moor Farm, whilst the former Devon longhouse and traditional stone buildings were left with Court Farm from where a successful bed and breakfast business was established. At that time four families lived and worked in the hamlet, each retaining at least some involvement in farming.

During the 1980s, Heale Farm was divided and the majority of its land sold as "off-ground" to an established farmer 9 miles away. Two of the traditional buildings were converted to provide holiday cottage accommodation while the remaining acres, comprising grazing, silage ground and the odd field of fodder beet, were used for a small dairy herd

At Higher Heale, a bungalow was built to accommodate the next generation while the house at Heale Moor farm was further extended and the attached land reduced to 25 acres. Similarly, land was sold at Court Farm where only one paddock was retained and traditional buildings were converted to provide more B&B rooms

In the 1990s, the almost derelict building that had been Heale Farm's house (it was destroyed by fire a century earlier) was reinstated. The replacement was sold to another family, with one field, creating Heale Barton. By now the small dairy herd could no longer provide a living and some arable crops were again grown on several Heale fields - oats with particular success but also barley, wheat and flax. But 70 acres was just not viable, so ground was sold off leaving 24 acres as Heale Farm plus two holiday cottages.

In 2003 there are nine dwellings in Heale. Six families live there permanently, one has a second home and visitors are constantly staying in the two holiday cottages. Two families are still farming as a full time occupation, with beef and sheep rearing the main enterprises, and all fields down to grass. The rest have other work or are retired.

In 1730 a lease drawn up for land at Heale compelled Richard Morris to pay £10 a year for five years to Henry Incledon for crops. With his signature Morris agreed to 'manage the land according to the best methods of husbandry'.

Reg Dallyn talking to George Court in his cattle lorry in 1954 .

5 Getting About

'The train waz zo vool es e could hold, an us waz zo thick es dress in a bed; an gwain round the cawnders us ed yessel agin wan tother. There waz a purty young umman next tu me, an her rather zimmed tu like it.'

For hundreds of years Parracombe stood in splendid isolation from its North Devon neighbours. Although this meant villagers were instinctively self-sufficient in their needs and entertainment the lack of decent transport links inevitably stifled commercial potential. It wasn't until the birth of tourism in the 18th century, and the patronage of Exmoor by Romantic poets such as Shelley (1792 - 1822) and Coleridge (1772 - 1834), that there was an upsurge of interest in the area and visitors began arriving in droves. At first the big winners were Barnstaple and, to a lesser extent, Lynton. But, gradually, better transport links helped Parracombe's tourist economy to blossom.

The Fox & Goose with a coach and four ready to go.

During the 19th century the horse-drawn coaches 'Tantivy', 'Glen Lyn and 'Tally Ho' plied their trade between Lynton and Barnstaple, passing through Parracombe en route. Fares for the trip - which took between three and four hours - were six shillings for a single journey or 10 shillings return. Each coach carried 20 passengers. At Loxhore the four horses pulling the carriage were changed and an extra animal was attached to ascend Loxhore Hill. A fifth horse was hitched to the coach at Parracombe to tackle the gradients while in winter a smaller three-horse carriage was used instead.

Coaches also ran between Ilfracombe and Lynton, coming to Parracombe every day except Sunday. The 'Benita' took three hours to negotiate the journey via Combe Martin and Kentisbury. Fares were between 4s and 7s.

John Latham, from Lyn Bridge, worked one of the coach routes through Parracombe. He left after securing a job at a livery stable and from there tried to forge a new life in America. He returned penniless in 1908 after his employer went bust, his wife had to go into service and he and his 10-year-old son faced the ignomony of the Barnstaple workhouse.

Six years later news came that Latham's former employer had come into an inheritance and could at last pay the wages he owed - in John's case the massive sum of £1025. Barnstaple Guardians' Committeee kept £425 and urged Latham to spend the rest of his money wisely. By now the last coach on the Barnstaple to Lynton route had already run, although the service from Ilfracombe continued.

In 1825 Britain's first passenger railway began operating between Stockton and Darlington and within 60 years the country was served by a 16,700-mile (26,900 kilometre) network of track. Unfortunately, none of it extended as far as Parracombe. It wasn't until 1898 that the Lynton & Barnstaple Railway opened and the village truly embraced the age of steam.

The L&B was initially financed by Derbyshire-born Sir George Newnes, who built a grand holiday home at Hollerday Hill in Lynton (later gutted by fire). He was publisher of Titbits and Country Life magazines as well as The Strand, in which Sherlock Holmes and Raffles stories first appeared. Sir George was a director of the Commonwealth Oil Corporation and a popular philanthropist who had already financed the Lynton-Lynmouth Cliff Railway and Lynton's electric street lighting. Later he would bankroll Lynton's magnificent and picturesque Town Hall.

There was an early dispute between Parracombe landowners and the railway company, probably over the price demanded for the land needed for the track. Ill-feeling was such that Parracombe was denied a full station and trains did not stop at all for the first year of the railway's operation. This antagonism was reflected in local reports of its official opening on 11th May 1898 but the acrimony eventually subsided and Parracombe soon had an operational station halt at Churchtown. It became valued as a water stop, allowing trains heading for Lynton to be fully charged ready for the steep coastal gradients ahead.

Laying the tracks was a demanding task. The cutting at Rowley Cross, about half a mile long, took over 18 months to complete and cost more than £5,000. To accommodate the demanding contours of the land a narrow gauge railway was planned, like the one at Festiniog in North Wales. This construction work had quite an impact on Parracombe, not least because of the influx of labourers. Here are some of the goings-on as reported by the local press.

Now rebuilt and remarketed as 'The Family & Commercial Hotel' with the Ilfracombe to Lynton stagecoach just arrived.

Parracombe Halt can still be found at the top end of Church Lane, but unfortunately without rails or platform.

Among the first to have his collar felt was navvy Henry Clarke. He was sentenced to a month's imprisonment with hard labour for taking 5s 1 1/2d and a half pence from the pocket of Charles Hutchings, who was fast asleep in the Fox & Goose. Then there was Samuel Galliford, given seven days with hard labour after being caught red-handed with a loudly-clucking hen. Galliford, a navvy from Torrington, admitted he'd been drinking beer before he stole it from Mr G Rattenbury.

Labourer William Allen, 45, was sentenced to six months hard labour for stealing two boxes of cigars, one bottle of brandy, two bottles of whisky and other articles from Henry Robert Blackmore. Another railway navvy was fined two shillings and six pence for smashing a quart jug at the Fox & Goose. One court report quoted a prosecuting lawyer, Mr W A Roberts, as saying that Mr Blackmore 'had a bad lot to deal with at Parracombe just now'. It seems the senior local police officer, Sergeant Adams, had his hands full!

Despite all this the opening of the railway was voted a success. The local paper's Parracombe correspondent reported proceedings as follows:

'Hundreds of folks drove over from here to Lynton to meet the train, notwithstanding the excessively cold weather and gloomy aspect which in the afternoon developed into heavy showers. The elements certainly were against the pleasure-seekers although everything passed off very nicely. The fireworks, however, were so damp that a part of them proved rather a failure.

'Sir George Newnes in the course of his speech, referred to the exorbitant price paid for the land and as some Parracombe folks opposed this railway the remark may be thought to refer to us, but if the valuer, Mr Smyth Richards, were consulted I think it would be shown that no high charges were asked here. Only one landowner, I believe, threatened to go to law and the result was that he obtained less than the company at first offered him.'

Top o'Mucksy Lane

Passengers who picked up the train at the unmanned Parracombe halt - at first a simple wooden shelter - could buy their tickets at the local post office before trekking up the hill to Churchtown. It took an hour and three quarters for the train to get from Barnstaple to Lynton (a distance of some 19 miles) but tickets were competitively priced and it saved at least an hour on the coach journey. In addition to the Parracombe stop locals would sometimes use the stations at Woody Bay and Blackmoor Gate.

On high days and holidays the carriages could get rather packed. Jim Slocum, writing from his address at 'top o'Mucksy Laane, Parrycum', says as much in a letter to the North Devon Journal detailing his trip to Barnstaple Fair in about 1899:

> *'Dear Zur*
> *I went in tu Bastabul Vair last Vriday, zo I thort I'd like tu telle how I got awn and how I didn't get awn.*
> *Years ago us useted tu draive in way a long-tail cart, an a bundle ov straw, but now us ken go be train, if us ken only manage tu git up zo vurs Blackmoor Geat.*
> *The train waz zo vool es e could hold, an us waz zo thick es dress in a bed; an gwain round the cawnders us ed yessel agin wan tother. There waz a purty young umman next tu me, an her rather zimmed tu like it.'*

In the same year it was reported that about 25 people used Parracombe Halt station on a Monday and that Fridays were also very busy. Indeed, Parracombe seemed to be enjoying the best of both worlds, according to the local correspondent in 1899.

'The railway appears to have had a depressing effect on some of the villages between Barnstaple and Lynton which were formerly enlivened by the coaches. Parracombe does not suffer so much from this as the coaches from Ilfracombe seem now to be on the increase.'

A Londoner, J Hartnoll, wrote about his trip on the Lyn-Barn railway in the Brixtonian, delighted at the punctuality of the service.

'In going to Lynton by rail it is necessary to give a word of warning, not to get too close to the engine. Though a small 'puffing billy' it emits an enormous quantity of black smoke and specks of soot which fills the nearest carriages with a sulphurous odour most objectionable to persons having broncial effections....

Barnstaple & Lynton railway adjacent to the Parracombe bypass.

'Ten years ago one would have thought it impossible to get from Barnstaple to Lynton for 1s 7½d but this is the fare today by all the trains, in contradistiction to 10s or more by the coach of former times. The trains per day are not numerous. Five up and five down, at rather long interval. This gives plenty of opportunity to the porters to cultivate the platform gardens and pick out the names of the stations with white 'dappy stones'. Another season some novel effects in foliage may be anticipated.'

Railway staff were clearly held in some affection by local people. This account was given of one man's departure from Blackmoor Gate within two years of the station's opening:

'On Tuesday evening Mr Henry Sowden, station master at Blackmoor Gate was presented with a public testimonial on leaving to take a position on the Westward Ho! Railway. The gift consisted of a cruet stand accompanied by a framed address (beautifully printed by Mr P Harris of High Street, Barnstaple).

The address was as follows: "We the undersigned desire to express our appreciation of your courtesy while station master at Blackmoor Station. We therefore ask your acceptance of this address and the accompanying cruet stand and wish you every success in your new post".'

In the late twenties Marjorie Bray (nee Smyth) recalls taking the train from Parracombe to Barnstaple, a journey of at least an hour. 'As Parracombe only had a halt mother had to get off the train at Blackmoor Gate to buy the tickets. I used to be petrified the train would go without her.'

Later the author Henry Williamson, creator of 'Tarka the Otter', wrote often about his trips on the railway and refers to one quaint village custom in his essay 'On Foot in Devon' published in 1933.

'From Blackmoor Gate the line swings to the right to avoid the great dip which leads down into the village of Parracombe. Until the loop road was made the hill was considered dangerous for cyclists and motorists, for it went straight down to the village itself and there was a sharp right-handed turn at the bottom by a cottage. There was talk of widening the road and of doing away with some of the cottages, but fortunately it was decided to cut a new loop road to take the thousands of motorcoaches which pass here every day in the summer.

'The new road runs beside the railway, and joins the old road half a mile beyond and above Parracombe.

'The village is a good one for the hiker. Let the motors grind themselves to death on the concrete loop in the distance, while for you, if you can find it, there is an inn where you may get what nowadays is very rare - genuine home-brewed beer. This home-brew tastes of beer. It has none of that metallic bitter taste which the townsman is said to approve, and which is only saltpetre, fermented glucose and other chemicals.

'If you visit the inn in cold weather, when a fire is burning, get the poker red hot in the embers (avoiding tar smoke) and plunge it into your beer. It's an old custom hereabouts.'

The engines pulling carriages along the Lyn-Barn line were named Yeo, Exe, Taw and Lyn. The Lew was added after the line was taken over by Southern Railways in 1923, at a cost of £38,000. Despite investment by the new owners, including a concrete halt at Parracombe, the steam train could not compete with cars and motor coaches using a vastly improved road network. A deputation from Parracombe and Lynton fighting the closure of the line met for last-ditch talks with line owners in Barnstaple. They turned up to the crunch meeting in their cars. The last train ran on 29th September 1935.

Still, Parracombe people remained hopeful that rail would return to the district. Following a meeting held at Blackmoor Gate Hotel during the Second World War, parish councillors united with counterparts on Lynton Urban District Council to lobby Great Western Railway for a new branch to link Filleigh Station with Blackmoor Gate. However, their efforts came to nothing and, indeed, the outlook for Filleigh Station itself was bleak.

Wretched roads

The age of motoring came late to Parracombe. One early motorist, Mrs Rodolph Stawell, explains why in her 'Motor Tours of the West Country': 'Through Parracombe, where there are two hills of some renown, a descent and a climb. The inconvenience here is in the fact that the change from the downwards to the upward gradient is in the middle of the village and a run is out of the question. The road surface here is described by others as 'wretched'.'

Not until 1919 did charabancs appeared in numbers. Travellers who came by train to Barnstaple before catching the coach to Lynton were often scared witless by the descent into Parracombe and roads around the village were notoriously poor. In April 1898 Scott's Royal Circus arrived for the first time in years and Sunday School children were treated to an outing by their superintendant. But circus proprietor Mr Scott was critical of the state of the road into the village and there's no record of him returning.

The local paper's correspondent highlighted the problems shortly afterwards: 'Cyclists are fond now-a-day of riding without brakes, which results frequently in accidents and narrow escapes while descending our almost perpendicular hills. At present however there is no such danger there being more likelihood of the cyclists sticking in the mud as it lies so very deep on the roads.' Given such conditions it's unsurprising that cars were a rare sight in Parracombe. The first villager to buy one, in 1924, was Mr Kinsey of Lorna Doone.

Soon cars rather than coaches, trains or cycles, brought visitors to the village. After the Second World War Ted Harris, who ran a taxi firm in East Down, did fine business by transporting visitors from Barnstaple to Mill Farm for cream teas.

Ships have played a small, but fascinating, part in the history of Parracombe as a number of young men chose to go away to sea above agriculture or the army. But the most poignant story concerns William Dovell, born in Parracombe on 30th October 1806 into a prominent local family. In 1964 local historian John Slader wrote about the young William in the North Devon Journal.

'Often he could be found near Heddon's Mouth, watching the sailing schooners unloading their cargoes of limestone. He would meet sailors in the kitchen bar of the old thatched farmhouse which later became the Hunters' Inn.

'Through adjoining fields he often walked to the highest point on Martinhoe Common. There his eyes would follow the great East Indiamen as they sailed by on their way to Bristol Dock.'

William married Frances Quartly from Molland and together they had a son, also called William. He achieved his ambition of going to sea, becoming a captain and moving to Bristol when it was one of England's busiest ports. Unusually, when Captain Dovell's ship the *Adelaide* set sail in the Autumn of 1850, both Frances and young William were aboard. Perhaps she hoped the bracing sea air would ease the boy's 'weak chest'.

An alternative method of transport which required much concentration and not a little co-operation. Left to right: Ivor Harding, Bill Worth, Roy Worth and Claude Rogers late 1940s.

There's evidence that they left with a heavy heart. Frances apparently told her neighbours that she feared they would never return. The tone of the voyage had been set when two sailors drowned trying to fix a faulty rudder as the ship prepared to sail.

If Frances did have a premonition it proved correct. On the morning of 19th December the ship foundered off the northwest coast of Spain at Laxe, near Coruna, and among the 16 who died were Frances and her son. Captain Dovell buried his wife's body on unconsecrated ground close to Laxe church (at the time it was illegal for Protestants like Frances to be buried in a Catholic cemetery). The body of young William was washed up some days later alongside other crew members.

According to local tradition in Laxe the grief-stricken captain for years returned to roam the village and churchyard, always carrying a bible under each arm. A decade later he re-married and returned to live in Barnstaple. As to the *Adelaide*, divers are still recovering items from her wrecked remains.

6 The Great Silver Rush

'...There is little or no doubt the mine will prove itself to be one of the most profitable yet worked in Devon.'

Perhaps silver 'rush' isn't quite the right term. However a browse through the mining journals of late Victorian England suggests that shafts and tunnels were being dug at the very heart of Parracombe in the belief that silver production was commercially viable. Even allowing for the boundless enthusiasm of mine owners in talking up prospects, a standard tactic for attracting outside investors, it seems that this work continued underground for up to two years.

The presence of the silver-lead ore galena (which can be smelted to extract pure silver) beneath Parracombe is hardly surprising. The village stands on the same rock beds that proved so profitable for Combe Martin mines down the centuries and during Elizabethan times these were the most productive in England. But what is slightly mystifying is that so much time, hope, effort and money was put into an operation which, in the end, proved such a flop. It is also curious that so little oral, written or visible evidence of the mining operation has survived.

So what *do* we know of Parracombe's 'lost' mine. The discovery of silver in the village was made in 1876 when, according to White's Directory of Devonshire (1878)... 'in digging the foundations for the brewery in 1876 silver ore was found.'. The brewery was located near the bottom of what we today call the Tarr Path.

After this, things moved apace according to reports in the *Mining Journal*. Frustratingly, the identities and roles of the authors are not always clear, site descriptions are vague and the terminology can be downright confusing (see glossary at the end of this chapter). However from talking to North Devon mines historian Mike Warburton, who has kindly passed his research on to us, it seems the initial main shareholder and founding mine captain (foreman) was one Charles Henry Maunder of Combe Martin.

It is thought Maunder was employed in the Combe silver mines but, either because he fell out with his employers or wished to own his own mine, by 1877 he was overseeing operations at Parracombe. He and his family are later recorded in the 1881 census for North Bovey, Dartmoor, where they lived at the East Vitifer Mine.

Charles Henry Maunder, 33, tin miner/mine agent born Stoke Climsland, East Cornwall
Isabella Maunder, 30, wife born St Blazey, Cornwall
Elizabeth Mable Maunder, 4, born Combmartin, Devon
Winnifred B I Maunder, 1, born Stoke Climsland, Cornwall

We know only fragments of Maunder's story but at least we do have extracts from some 19th century mining journals and newspapers as recorded by Dr Peter Claughton, author of *A List of Mines in North Devon & West Somerset*. In the references below 'MJ' refers to the *Mining Journal*, 'NDJ' is the *North Devon Journal* and 'MSHO' is the *Mineral Statistics Home Office Report*.

MJ 3.2.1877

S.R.B *[unidentified organisation]* meeting at the Royal London Hotel, Parracombe to meet many friends. Inspected the balance sheet which astonished me when I saw the rich lode of Ag/Pb [silver lead] at so shallow a depth. The adit being driven to intersect the lode further west where we expect to find rich Ab/Pb lode. What a splendid spot for a mine.

MJ 21.7.1877

Combmartin District: East Combmartin (Parracombe)

The grant of this property is to be obtained and shortly to be started on the cost book system. The lodes in this property have already been sufficiently developed to ensure success. (RK)

MJ 13.10.1877

Parracombe: An extensive grant has been obtained by a very influential mining proprietary for the purpose of working the rich silver lead lode accidentally discovered in sinking a well on the premises of the Parracombe Brewery. The lode so far as seen is 4ft wide.

MSHO Report 1877

Parracombe Ag/Pb - Charles Maunder & Co. Mine captain C.H. Maunder.

MJ 19.1.1878

Parracombe Ag/Pb on 6 a crosscut has been driven and timbered for 15 fathoms. 1 lode intersected and 10 fathoms already in its course. Higher backs obtained, lode regular 4ft wide gossan and quartz, flooken, spar, mundic Cu Ag/PB of a very rich quality and improves in depth. Mine a complete success. *[This report suggests a horizontal tunnel, supported by wooden props, was dug for some 90ft. The miners then struck a promising seam of silver lead and followed it in a new direction for a further 60ft. The quality of the ore got better the deeper they went. The names given are minerals associated with silver deposits - Ed.]*

MJ 2.3.1878

Parracombe: We understand that work will shortly be resumed under the direction of a company.

NDJ 21.3.1878

Parracombe: The mining operations have been suspended here since the beginning of March.

MJ 29.3.1878

Parracombe Silver Lead Mining Co.

A preliminary meeting of the shareholders was held at Exeter on 29th March (sic) when the reports of the mining captains were read and highly approved of. The shareholders may well congratulate themselves upon the acquirement of this valuable sett, as there is little or no doubt the mine will prove itself to be one of the most profitable yet worked in Devon. It is always a good feature when the shares are applied for by the public in the immediate neighbourhood and this is notably the case with this mine, as from the list of shares taken up, laid upon the table, it appears that about 80% are held by Gentlemen living in that neighbourhood. The following report by Capt. Stenlake was read at the meeting. *(Capt Stenlake was presumably a mining surveyor - Ed.)*

'At your request I have inspected the property known as the Parracombe Silver Lead Mine, situated in the parish of Parracombe, North Devon, about 3 miles to the East and on the same lodes as the celebrated Combmartin mine from which large quantities of Silver Lead have been sold.

At Parracombe there are eight lodes traversing the sett, which is about three-quarter of a mile in length and half a mile wide. On the North West side of the stream an adit crosscut has been driven north about 15 fathoms and has intersected the No.1 lode, this drivage has been continued on its course 10 fms East and for this distance the lode is from 2 to 3 ft wide, composed of quartz, carbonate of lime, mundic and silver lead ore, from an opening made in this lode 15 fms to the East of the present end, good stones of lead ore have been taken up and as the adit advances towards this point Have (sic) no doubt but that a profitable lode will be met with.

On the South side of the stream an adit level has been taken up on No.5 lode and been driven on its course 4 to 5 fathoms; in the present end the lode is 2ft wide with a very promising appearance composed chiefly of beautiful gossans, quartz, and stones of lead ore by extending this adit West backs of from 25 to 30 fms will be gained and from its present appearance large quantities of lead will be met with.

The facilities you have for working this property are very favourable, as you have an excellent stream of water running through the sett available for pumping and dressing purposes. I would recommend a shaft being sunk on No.1 lode, and as depth is obtained in my opinion a profitable lode will be met with and that the adit be driven West on No 5 lode as I think this is a very important point. In conclusion I would remark that you have a property of great value, and if vigorously worked with judicious management a very small capital will in my opinion make it a good lasting mine.

(From these March 1878 extracts we can conclude that work on Parracombe Mine had been temporarily halted, presumably to form a new company and inject working capital. Already a tunnel totalling some 150ft deep had been dug 'north west' of the Heddon and confidence in the worked lode seems to have been high. That said, it is rare for any report of entrepreneurial mining operations to be pessimistic! The problem we have is pinning down the areas mentioned. Any glance at a map shows that the Heddon runs roughly southeast to northwest through the village. What precisely does Captain Stenlake mean then by 'the North West side of the stream'? Ed.)

MJ 11.5.1878

Letters to the Editor - Parracombe Silver Lead.

Sir,

A few days since I paid a visit to this valuable sett and probably the following notes will interest those of your readers who have taken an interest in this property as well as those wondering about so doing. I was particularly struck with its beautiful situation, being in the southern slope of the hill, and offering such advantages for driving on the courses of the lodes as are but seldom met with.

The geological character of the strata is all that could be desired for the production of silver lead whilst numerous lodes and their length of over 200 fathoms show most clearly the ample content of the mineral resources at the command of the company and this is an important consideration in connection with the success of any mine. An excellent stream of water running through the property is an advantage not to be overlooked in estimating the probable profits of this mine, as here the saving of capital which is usually expended in steam power will most materially increase the percentage of the dividends which I predict will not only be large but also an early result.

Since my last visit a cross course has been intersected in the adit driven on the course of Lode Number 1 at this point the lode is not only wider but also richer and a very promising indication for the future; altogether this is a well-defined and masterly lode and as an extra staff of men are put to work at this point I fully expect 'ere long to hear of good results. Number 5 lode on the south side of the stream has a most promising appearance composed of beautiful gulsen, quartz and stones of lead ore and from 3 - 4ft wide and by extending this adit west backs of [many?] more fathoms will quickly be gained and from its appearance I believe large quantities of lead ore will be met with. Judging from this it is a valuable and masterly one.

From this point also I brought out some good stones containing copper and lead. After an inspection lasting over three hours I drove back to the station with a conviction most strongly confirmed in my mind that ultimately Parracombe Mine will rank as one of the most prosperous ones in the county and that the company may

fully expect to meet with the reward they so well deserve (sic).
May 9th, R J Rutter.

MJ 15.5.1878
Parracombe: In driving the East crosscourse 4ft in width Blue Killas, flakes of Mundic, and Ag/Pb. 20-30 fathoms on the line of the lode very rich Ag/Pb near the surface. Sinking on West lode doing well. Quarts (sic), Barytes, Mundic, Copper, and Silver Lead and better the deeper we go. No. 5 lode as before. Backs to be gained of about 35-40 fathoms with good spots of Ag/Pb.

MJ 15.6.1878
Parracombe. Good progress. No.1 lode good Ag/Pb lode rich Ag rich and lasting ore half a ton of ore per fathom. No.2 lode 6ft wide nearly 8ft deep rich copper and lead encouraging.

MJ 28.6.1878
Parracombe. No.1 lode East half a ton of good Ag/Pb per fathom. The lode West continues to improve, large quantities of Ag/Pb ore just on top rich ore East and West of the cross course, press on ahead.

MJ 13.7.1878
Parracombe No.1 lode is still half a ton of Ag/Pb per fathom the lode is opening well *[unknown symbol]* Cu, Mundic, Blend and Ag/Pb. *[We are going]* to start a new dip adit to intersect No.2 lode.

...On Monday we commenced to drive the deep adit level to intersect the No.2 lode.

MJ 27.7.1878
Parracombe Deep *[Ed's note; definitely not Dip]* adit extended to cut No.2 lode Mundic, Cu Blend, Ag/Pb as good as last time, very cheering.

MJ 24.8.1878
We are driving on the No.1 lode it is 6-7ft wide, rich silver lead 30 fms long

And there the *Mining Journal's* record of operations at Parracombe abruptly and mysteriously ends. Did Maunder and his company run out of money? Was the ore of poorer quality than suggested? Was there a problem attracting labour? Given the excitement and frequency of reports between March and August 1878 it seems a curious way to close a venture which apparently promised so much. The official Mineral Statistics record sheds little light, revealing only that in 1878...

'Parracombe Ag/Pb: 4 males over 16 working underground none above. Parracombe Mining Co. Mine Captain F.E. Young'.

'Jo' Constable guarding and demonstrating the scale of an adit at Twineford (or Tynerdy)

The 1879 Mineral Statistics record is the same but in 1880 the telling words 'not worked' are added. All we can say for sure is that frantic activity was reported at Parracombe Mine during the spring and summer of 1878. This may have continued into 1879, although Maunder and his investors were strangely silent on progress. By 1880 work had been abandoned, presumably with the company and its shareholders facing heavy debts.

However Maunder stubbornly refused to abandon hopes of a return on his investment. In a letter written 20 years later to one A.E. Doidge of Callington, Cornwall - reprinted in *Adventurers Slopes* by Douglas Stucky (1965) - he writes in glowing terms of Parracombe Mine's potential. Maunder does not make clear whether he still legally owns the mineral rights but he certainly paints a rosy picture.

'The above mining property is situated in the parish of Parracombe, North Devon. One mile from the railway station.The grant is very extensive and contains three or more well known Silver Lead lodes. A continuation of the Combmartin Silver Lead lodes.

'No 1 lode was discovered by the stream close to the surface an open cutting, and driving of a tunnel West some few fathoms on the line of the lode proved the same to be from two to four feet in thickness, composed chiefly of beautiful Gossan, Quarts (sic), Copper, Zinc and Silver Lead ore.

'An assay has been made proving the ore worth fifteen and three quarters in twenty, equal to Seventy eight and Three quarters percent for Lead, and Twelve and a half ounces of fine Silver to the ton. *[How valuable would this make the mine? The problem, says Mike Warburton, is 'per ton of what?' However he believes that 'as old systems of ore analysis go, it was pretty good if they could have found enough of it.' Ed.]*

'Tunnel. The driving of the Tunnel West will quickly gain backs from about 200 to 240 feet from the surface and the great depth, and length to be obtained on this lode is highly favourable for successful working.

'There are two other strong lodes which have been examined and proved to traverse the entire length of the property, and are good indications of two other valuable lodes which in my opinion can be opened on, almost immediately.

Strata. The killas stratification of the property these lodes traverse is exactly the same mineralised character as in the Combmartin mines, from which have been sold Silver Lead ore to the value of $602,200.

The facilities for vigorous development with a moderate capital can scarcely be excelled, considering the many substantial advantages for developing the different lodes by tunnels, the great value of waterpower for all purposes, also near rail and shipping for cheap transit for all material and minerals. I am fully convinced it is a property of great value and with judicious management the working will be very profitable.

Yours truly, C.H. Maunder, M.E.
Torquay
20th November 1900.

Sadly for Maunder, nobody else shared his dream and Parracombe Mine became a fading memory. The Tarr Path shaft and an adjoining adit is however recorded in a 1993 Royal Commission on the Historical Monuments of England field survey which states that: '...From the west side of a field bank some 10m to the west of the shaft in a pasture field is a linear trench. It is 4m wide, 0.4m deep and runs for some 23m south west to the edge of the old river terrace of the River Heddon. It appears to be a collapsed adit into the shaft.'

Today some residents still recall a story told by the late George Smyth, of West Bodley, who remembered burning rubbish in the shaft as a child. This caused an explosion brought about by a rush of air from beneath! History group members have recently tried to uncover the shaft but the site has been infilled and is now heavily overgrown.

If the records are correct, there may also be a mine entrance and adit somewhere on the west bank of the Heddon, between the river and what is now Heale Road. It may even lie in somebody's garden!

Other known mines in the area

In 2003 Mike Warburton accompanied members of PAHG down a partially flooded adit higher up the Heddon Valley on land near Twineford, roughly 1km to the south of Parracombe. This is another silver-lead working, probably unrelated to Maunder's efforts further downstream. Mr Warburton believes it was most likely a one or two man operation, perhaps dating back several hundred years.

Precise measurements and rock analysis have still to be carried out but, as a rough guide, this adit runs straight into the hillside for some 15 metres, turning sharp left at a point where the miners decided to follow a silver-lead seam. It then continues for a further 12 metres to a dead-end.

Finally, according to *Mining Regions of South West England* (Vol. II), there is a trial shaft some 1.5 miles north-northeast of Parracombe. Thirty yards from this shaft, which was probably sunk to find iron ore or lead, is an adit entrance.

Glossary of mining terms

Adit: Horizontal tunnel.

Ag/Pb: Silver-lead

Assay: Test for metal quality

Backs: Workings above the adit, following the slope of the lode

Barytes: Mineral

Blend: Mineral

Cu: Copper

Cost book system: A forerunner of the limited liability company in which a group of entrepreneurs would agree a start-up figure and advertise shares, usually at around £2 per share. There would be an understanding that further calls for capital would be made up to a guaranteed annual limit, perhaps £1 per share. Shareholders who failed to respond would forfeit their interests

Although this system was a good way of raising money for mining ventures its flaw was that investors received a dividend as soon as the mine made a profit. This was often exactly the time profits needed to be re-invested. No wonder small mines (like Parracombe!) faced the constant threat of closure.

Driveage: Tunnel or Tunnelling

Flooken clay: As distinct from alluvial clay. Mineral-like substance found within a lode.

Gossan quartz: Surface rocks from which the quartz has been leached by water. The quartz is usually re-deposited deeper in the lode.

Gulsen: Mineral.

Killas stratification: In North Devon this referred to slates and sandstones lying beneath the northeast side of the Combe Martin valley. The fact that at Parracombe these rocks were adjacent to limestone offered the possibility of significant silver lead deposits.

Lode: Rock containing metal ore.

Mundic: The meaning of this word changes according to different generations and areas. Here it probably meant arseno pyrite.

Sett or Set: Mining area.

Spar: A Devon word for quartz.

7 Saving Souls

'One of the match tops landed in the beard of the Sunday School teacher. We all watched horrified as a wisp of smoke curled up from his beard, expecting him to go up in flames like Moses and the burning bush.'

At the turn of the century, a family leave Hunter's Inn going up the Heddon Valley towards Parracombe.

St Petrock's Church is dedicated to a Cornish saint famous for sheltering a hunted stag. Petrock is supposed to have died at Bodmin on 4th June 564 and it may be that a humble church was raised in his name at Parracombe during or soon after his lifetime (see also Chapter 1).

If so, a substantial stone church replaced it in the 11th century, probably funded by William de Falaise. The tower was added later in 1182 and one theory is that this work was financed by one of St Thomas Becket's killers as a penance for the blood shed. Becket was Archbishop of Canterbury when he quarrelled with King Henry II on ecclesiastical matters. He was killed in Canterbury Cathedral in 1170 by four Royal courtiers convinced they were carrying out the will of the monarch.

Inside St Petrock's it appears that the chancel dates to 1252 while the font is almost certainly medieval and perhaps even older. Having been abandoned in the Rectory gardens at Martinhoe it was given to St Petrock's by the rector, the Rev Reginald Oldham in 1908. The building as we know it today was largely re-constructed in the late 15th or early 16th century and in late Victorian times the bells were removed to be re-hung in the 'new' church - Christchurch. The only bell now remaining in the tower is almost modern by comparison, having been supplied by Mears and Stainbank in 1908.

In a 1902 edition of Kelly's Trades Directory St Petrock's - one of eight churches in Devon which bear the name. - is referred to as St Peter's while a map dated 1890 names it as St Helen's. At some time there was supposedly a banner or shield bearing the name St Helen's Church, Parracombe, although nobody knows it whereabouts today.

The church was a target of Puritans soon after the English Civil War and two of its bells - originally donated by the St Aubyn family - were melted down, presumably deemed too ostentatious. The bells were refounded shortly afterwards and one is inscribed 'Will Mortymer, James Graden (Wardens) T.P.,I.P.,1669'. A second bell with a diameter of nearly a metre (35.5 inches) is inscribed 'Richard Bale, John Greene, 1653'. The third bell bears the words: 'John Bunt, Richard Harton, Churchwardens, 1743. T. Wroth.' The final name is that of a man in Goodleigh who recast the bell.

There's little known of Civil War action in Parracombe although a sword and canon ball were discovered at Newbery fields. Perhaps Puritans sought vengeance on other church furnishings although some carved oak benches seem to have survived that era. The later 'horse-box' pews were probably from Georgian times, designed to eliminate draughts for the vulnerable church-goer. St Petrock's is also said to be the last church in Devon where musicians were employed. They sat in the raised pews at the back, one of which bears a hole cut to accommodate the bow of a bass viol.

The screen, with its painted panels, was made before 1758 when church accounts reveal that £1 11s 6d was paid for the cleaning of the Commandments.

It is assumed the painting of the Royal Arms inscribed G R dates from the reign of George I (r1714-27) while the sundial over the porch is clearly inscribed 1726, suggesting the church interior has hardly changed at all in 300 years.

Churchwardens' accounts from the Georgian period have yielded some fascinating details. The churchwardens were principal officers of the parish and their duties were mainly connected with the maintenance and repair of church property, killing vermin, dealing with vagrants, paying wages and expenses for various officers and witnessing the

The 11th century St Petrock's Church, showing the rood screen and pulpit. The church is also well known for its horse-box pews.

registration of baptisms, marriages and burials etc. The records reflect this wide range of responsibilities.

In 1712 the cost of bread and wine for five communions at St Petrock's amounted to £1 14s. Thomas Harris was paid 8d for killing four fiches, an old term for polecats. The dog whipper, whose job it was to keep dogs out of the church, earned five shillings from church funds while the fox catcher was paid eighteen shillings for his efforts. A shilling was paid for a bundle of laths and 6d for a bushel of Welsh lime. The wages of the clerk amounted to £1 13s 4d.

By 1735 Richard Crang and William Harton were church wardens and had £10 7s 2d to spend, a relatively large sum taken out of the rates. Entries in their ledger for that year include 5s for two bell ropes, 8s for the bell ringers and 2s to Elizabeth Coneber for cleaning the church. One item accounts for 8s for 'ye rejoicing day for ye King'. This was during the reign of George II (1727-60) although the purpose and form of the celebration remains unknown.

Accounts from both years refer to paying for 'passes'. This refers to an old system of government control over the movement of the poor. Those without means had to obtain a pass from a vicar or magistrate which entitled them to small sums of cash from the officials of parishes on their route. Frequently seamen were the beneficiaries of this system.

In the accounts of 1742 the first item was a shilling 'allowed myselfe for going to Loxhore for to send a letter to the Belfounder at the City of Gloster.' The foundryman he summoned travelled to Parracombe where the churchwardens spent 11s on ale for him. It is possible that he founded the bell in the village rather than transported it from his own workshop.

The following year the records reveal that 1s 6d was 'for myselfe for going to Ilfordcombe to spicke with Mr John Goss about the bell'. A further 1s 6 d went to the church warden for removing the existing bell as well as three shillings for three others to help. The belfounder was paid £11 13s for the job. One entry for 1744 notes that the resident dog-whipper was a woman and that she was paid 5s for her trouble.

For many years it was possible to purchase a seat in the chancel and, in the 18th century, this cost 1s and 6d or 2s. The parish was expected to pay 5s yearly to the Rector to reserve seats for the Excise Officer and his family in the chancel.

Ringers' ale

In 1760 4s was paid for ale to refresh the bellringers during celebrations for the accession of George III. The ale in question was almost certainly brewed at Church Cottage. Two years later the records reveal that a black and gold lace cloth or decoration was hung in the pulpit.

Among items recovered in research for this book were` St Petrock's Vestry minutes between 1813 and 1854. From these we learn that a church committee played a major part in village life. It was responsible for appointing churchwardens, overseers, constables (on behalf of the district magistrates) and surveyors of the highway. At a meeting held on 17 April 1830 parishioners met to appoint a Sexton. Among his tasks was to chime the bells, wash the church once a year, clean up outside the church and 'anything else the rector wishes'. William Slader was given the job at a rate of one pound per year.

The group also met regularly to set a poor rate and a church rate, presumably to be exacted from local people.

On 7 June 1830 parishioners agreed that the sum of £15 should be taken from the Church rate to build a vestry room in the church yard. John Pyke, who chaired the meeting, was backed by eight other signatories.

The following entry is printed as it appears, to illustrate that accurate spelling was not a big issue at the time. This explains why place names and surnames vary - including the spelling of Parracombe itself.

> *August 4 1846*
> *A Publick vestery held at the vestery room on Tuesday the 4th day of August by two o'clock in the afternoon for the purpose of consulting about widening and repairing the road between Bodley Crofs and Paracombe Mill Bridge.*
> *At this meetting it was agreed that the road should be widenend between bodley crofs and Paracombe Mill. Also to break up the pitching in Paracombe Mill and crack the stones and laid on the said road.*

It was signed by James Smyth, (*chierman*), and five others.

The most extraordinary entry in the notebook showed the lengths town and village would go to in order to keep out so-called undesirables.

> *Parracombe December 28 1846*
> *The parish committee met 'to consider the prospect of appealing against an order made by W Avery and J Marshall, two justices of the Borough of Barnstaple, for the removal of Susan Blackmore singlewoman and her two Bastard children from the Parish of Barnstaple to the Parish of Parracombe. The Revd John Pyke in the chair.*
> *That the said order be appealed against and that the overseers of the poor of the said parish of Parracombe are authorised to employ W Bray or some other competent person to draw up a notice of appeal and to state the grounds of appeal against the said order and to take all necessary steps for prosecuting the said appeal at Quarter sessions.'*

In 1916 a copy was made of gravestone and church inscriptions. This shows the slab in the floor of the chancel, directly in front of the altar, was decorated with a Lombardic cross and dedicated to a former rector, probably Sir Edmund Hole who died in 1377. It's also clear that the church has had some close calls over the years - a brief paragraph in a commerical directory and gazeteer of Devonshire, dated 1870, tells how it was partly destroyed by a fire on 19th December 1869.

In his local history notes Arthur Smyth records that St Petrock's once had a harmonium and a stove but observes that: '. . . there is nothing here in the graveyard to excite the curiosity of the antiquarian.'

He then offers the following anecdote: 'Near the porch will be seen the Dovell's of Killiton vault, and the names of twin brothers. At their birth, the excise officer said that owing to a certain planet under which they were born, one would die in childhood and the other scarcely live to the age of manhood. This stone tells how correct his prophecy was.' *[William Dovell died on 27th March 1805 aged nine days while his twin John died on 17th July 1824, before his 20th birthday - Ed.]*

Christchurch, Parracombe's 'new' church in the heart of the village, dates from 1877

Smyth also informs us that St Petrock's was once used as a school but had since grown dilapidated. Certainly, by 1879 there were fears that it had become unstable and at risk of collapse, perhaps the lingering effects of the fire mentioned above. Initially, it was proposed that the existing church be demolished and a new one constructed on the same site. That provoked widespread opposition, led by British writer and critic John Ruskin (1819-1900), for it was already a vintage building.

Outraged that such 'an act of vandalism' was being contemplated, Ruskin offered £10 towards the construction of a new church on a different site if only the old church could be left in peace. His idea won the day and the result was Christchurch, built in the heart of the village. The cost was in the region of £3,000, raised by subscriptions, grants and the proceeds of village fundraising. It was intended that the old church should become a mortuary chapel.

Soon Christchurch fulfilled all the roles that once belonged to St Petrock's. According to Henry Blackmore the last wedding of the era to be held in the old church was that of Frances Blackmore to Reuben Winter, the exact date of which is unknown. However, the graveyard remained open until 1971 and includes the grave of William Leworthy, killed in the flood of August 1952.

Before the end of the 19th century Christchurch was subject to some extensive refurbishment. On 15th June 1899 four new bells were added to the two hanging in the tower of Christchurch, completing a programme of restoration.

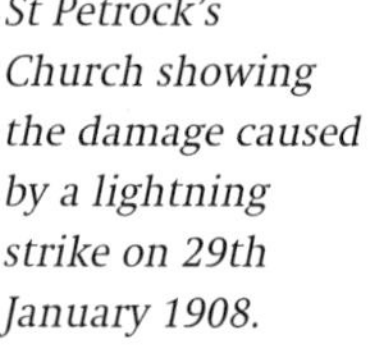

St Petrock's Church showing the damage caused by a lightning strike on 29th January 1908.

The range of bells are now as follows:

Treble F weighing four and a quarter cwt inscribed 'Gloria in Excelsis Deo 1899'
E weighing four and a half cwt inscribed 'we praise thee 1899'
D weighing five cwt, inscribed 'we bless these 1899'
C weighing five and a quarter cwt, dated 1669
B weighing six and a half cwt, inscribed 'we worship thee 1899'
Tenor note A, weighing eight and a half cwt, dated 1658

The Rev. John Chanter and churchwarden J Creek raised over £180 of the £200 charged by the London foundry, Mears and Stainbank. Tower repairs were carried out by Messrs Bryant and Son of Barnstaple. A ceremony held to mark the installation of the new bells appears to have been a grand affair and among the guests were the Bishop of Crediton together with vicars from Challacombe, Loxhore, Bratton, Martinhoe, Bishops Tawton, Charles, Kentisbury and Combe Martin

After the service the Rev and Mrs Chanter held a tea party for 300 at the Rectory *[Heddon Hall]*, 'the spacious grounds and gardens being an ideal spot for a gathering on a warm summer afternoon', as the local newspaper put it. The report added: 'The rhodedendrums and azaleas in the long walks are just in full bloom and with the beautiful white flowing ash were much admired'.

In the marquee, tea was served by Mrs Chanter and her helpers Mrs Dallyn from Rowley Barton, Mrs Gammin from Halwell, Mrs Lock, Mrs Creek, the three Misses Smyth from Voley, Mrs Widden and Mrs Lancey. Throughout the afternoon the Combe Martin Band played a selection from its repertoire and the day concluded with a 7.30 festival evensong in Christchurch.

For St Petrock's however the future remained bleak. Particularly when, on 29th January 1908, local newspapers reported that it had been wrecked by a lightning strike.

'At Parracombe never within the memory of any living person has a thunderstorm caused such serious damage as the storm of yesterday. The old church of St Peter which stands on the hill about a quarter of a mile from the village and which has braved the storms of centuries, has sustained almost irrepairable damage. At about 11.30 there was an exceptionally vivid flash of lightning followed immediately by two distinct crashes of thunder, which appeared to shake the earth.

'One of the pinnacles and a large portion of the corner of the tower were torn away and a large quantity of masonry fell from the southern side of the tower, leaving a hole several feet square . . . one large stone weighing at least three quarters of an hundredweight was hurled over 100 ft from the church. . . the pulpit is splintered like matchwood and parts of the screen are splintered. In the east end there are large fissures in the walls which appear to be twisted out of shape. Nearly all the glass in the windows has been smashed.'

A tablet on the south side of the tower reads as follows: 'This tower, five windows, the East-end porch, roofs and Pulpit were injured by lightning on 28th Jan 1908 and were restored the same year by public subscription and a lightning conductor and bell were provided and Martinhoe's disused font brought here.'

The name of John Frederick Chanter, Rector, Robert St John Allison (aka Paddy)and John Creek, Churchwardens, appear below this inscription.

In 1935 there were further concerns about the state of St Petrock's and an expert was called in to examine the screen. Sculptor and carver Herbert Read, of Exeter, wrote: ' . . . I went to the church last week and carefully inspected the Screen. I find it is in a very bad state of repair and, unless it can be thoroughly restored, I would strongly recommend leaving it as it is.

'For your guidance, however, I would say that I

Freddie Leworthy scything the grass in the churchyard circa 1985.

estimate the cost of removing the Screen from the Church, cleaning off the paint and carefully restoring the decayed and missing portions, including the one new carved panel on the South side and parts of the others and taking back the Screen and refixing it in the church, about £60.'

It is not known whether the recommended repairs were carried out.

Although the Anglican Church was a wealthy organisation individual parishes often operated on tight budgets. The turn of the century had been an expensive time for the parish of Parracombe, what with the refurbishment of Christchurch, its four new bells and the storm repairs at St Petrock's. The sums of money involved could not have been easily raised solely through tea parties and raffles.

Perhaps this is one reason why on 13th September 1909 - 18 months after the lightning strike - the Rev Chanter sold off the village Post Office and adjoining cottage to Miss Mary Georgina Thompson. The deal raised £215 and although it is unclear whether the profit went to the Church Commissioners or the parish it's not unreasonable to assume that at least some of the money was used to offset the continuing cost of structural work at the two churches.

The conveyancing deed shows that Chanter was acting under powers given by the Glebe Lands Act of 1888 and that he had to obtain permission from the Board of Agriculture and Fisheries. He also needed the approval of the Bishop of Exeter and the Patron of the Rectory of Parracombe, a Barnstaple man by the name of Charles Edward Roberts (sic) Chanter. Most likely the two Chanters were related, although this is unclear from the deed.

Seven years later, Miss Thompson broke up the Post Office buildings, selling the main business premises to Miss Helena Crocombe and the adjoining cottage (now Dale View) to Frederick Richard Latham. Miss Thompson's witness on Miss Crocombe's conveyancing deed is Philip Noel Nind, a marine engineer of 27, Carlton Crescent, Southampton. The Ninds were at one time a Parracombe family and were related by marriage to the Rev. Chanter.

Fred Latham's garden seems to have been at the far southwest boundary of the glebe lands and, as we know from historian Arthur Smyth, this was where the entrance gates for the original 500-metre coach road to Heddon Hall were sited. You can still see the remains of the gateposts behind the telephone box.

Legal documents show that these transactions were carried out on 28th December 1916 and although no record has emerged of the amount agreed by Latham we know that Miss Crocombe paid £275 for the Post Office. This suggests a huge rise in its value at a time when the economic effects of the Great War were presumably biting hard. Clearly the price reflected the purchase of a business but, even so, Miss Thompson pocketed a healthy 28% profit of £60 on the Post Office, *plus* whatever she got for Dale View. It seems fast-rising property prices have been a fact of life in Parracombe for very many years.

When he died in 1939 at the age of 85 Rev Chanter's will was published in the pages of the Daily Telegraph. In it he reveals that he was a religious moderate. He left the Rectory of Parracombe to his daughter, Violet Nind, 'trusting that she will present to any vacancy of the living which may occur a good, sound Churchman without Papist or Protestant proclivities and will on no account allow the advowson (*right of presentation to a churchman*) to get into the hands of any Protestant trusts.'

To Parracombe Church he bequeathed a chalice and instructed that the income from some debentures held in the Lynton Water Company be distributed to members of the church choir upon the anniversary of his death. (The arrangement has now been ended.)

Before his death he was treasurer and prebendary of Exeter Cathedral and left £50 to the Friends of Exeter Cathedral. Various archaeological books and manuscripts were given to Exeter City Library. He left estate valued at £31,705 gross

Some assistance for the poor was administered through the Church. In Parracombe this included a parochial relief fund as well as interest on two different gifts made to the parish. In the returns made to Parliament in 1786 it was stated that David Berry 'in 1760 gave by will £5 for the day labourers of this parish' and that some unknown person gave a further £23 to the poor.

Interest from the combined amounts was distributed by churchwardens every Easter 'among poor labourers not receiving parochial relief in sums of a few shillings each, varying according to the numbers of their family'.

Vicars in Parracombe were, it seems, largely absent. In his introduction to the book 'Parracombe Baptisms, Marriages, Burials 1597-1836, Rev John Chanter points out that Rectors often had addresses elsewhere. Lancelot St Albyn, he says, spent just one Saturday in Parracombe during the lengthy spell that he was Rector (1762-1791).

Consequently, curates were important characters in the village. One in particular, Rev J Fosse, perplexes Chanter. ' . . it is related that after he had married a certain couple in the parish, they came up to the rectory and hour later and asked to be "unmarried", which so enraged the old gentleman that he gave notice the following Sunday: "There will be no more marriages in this parish by me - if you will get married you must get a parson for yourself."

'It appears from the register that this story is true for the couple who wanted to be unmarried are the last for whom he officiated; and though he remained in the parish many years after and there were many marriages for which he filled in the forms, the name of the officiating priest is never the Rev John Fosse. He is also said to have dropped the baby at a christening and to have refused to take another; and from the registers it appears that he did not personally administer the sacrament of baptism during the last few years that he was curate in charge.'

Records in the book indicate that sailor Thomas Fry and Nancy Blackmore, married in 1805, were the couple in question and that Ann Bale, daughter of John and Prudence, was the unfortunate baby in 1811. The Frys presumably resigned themselves to live with their error as the baptism records show their children Mary Ann Fry and Nicholas Blackmore Fry being christened in 1806 and 1808.

Besotted curate

From Arthur Smyth's 'History of Parracombe' we learn the Rev Fosse's life was shadowed by unhappiness. Smyth writes: 'There lived in the village a respectable spinster who had arrived at that time of life when a lady cares not to tell her age. She was possessed of a fair income derived from stocks and shares etc. and she was withal of goodly personal appearance, active and thrifty in her household duties, and attendant on Mr Fosse's ministry. The worthy curate was said to be very attentive to this 'maiden' but she, albeit secretly inclined and hopeful, would most innocently deny anything beyond friendly pastoral regard.

'One afternoon, without any preliminary beating round the bush, the Reverend gentleman abruptly demanded her hand and heart. The lady, rather startled, blushingly and coyly replied "No thankee", though, as she afterwards admitted, she needed further pressing and proper courting, when she would have yielded. When this news was carried to his Reverence he quietly shook his head and said he would not make the lady change her answer and cause her to tell a lie and so they both remained single to their deaths; but the lady was often heard to say she wished "No thankee" hanged many times.'

Rev Fosse, he says, was buried at Ilfracombe.

Later vicars played an important role in supporting the poor and needy and the Rev Peter Nettleton Leakey (in post between 1870 and 1881) seems to have taken his duties particularly seriously. Following the sudden death of headmaster John Lock in 1873 (see Chapter 8 School Report) he wrote in the following terms to a local newspaper.

'His widow is left totally unprovided for, and is too

delicate to earn her own livelihood. I shall most thankfully receive any donation on her behalf, or can it be paid for her to 'The Barnstaple Branch of the West of England and South Wales District Bank.'

He also wrote a letter to the North Devon Journal appealing for cash to help another parishioner:

'Sir, Noah Palmer, a highly respectable man of this parish in the 70th year of his age, has lately broken down in his work as postman, in which capacity for nearly 18 years he has delivered letters in this district, walking daily over 10 miles in very rough and hilly country. He is not entitled to a pension as he received only eight shillings and for some time six shillings a week. He can do but little for himself and a sick wife. He is a truly godly man and for over 30 years has acted as parish clerk in this parish. It is now proposed to purchase for him a small annuity. Donations will be gratefully received by Rev P N Leakey.'

(Records from St Petrock's indicate that Noah Palmer, illegitimate son of 25 year old Elizabeth Palmer, was baptised in 1807. Palmer married Maria Richards in 1834 and they had at least two children, Eliza, baptised in January 1835, and Helen, christened the following year.)

Rev Leakey was a well-meaning but often ineffectual man. It was his idea to demolish St Petrock's to provide building material for Christchurch. The idea was firmly rejected. He also promised no burials would take place at Christchurch, a pledge which evidently amounted to nothing. Concerned about the evils of alcohol Rev Leakey brought in Mr Francis Wood, a naval petty officer during the Crimean War, to manage a temperance (non-alcoholic) hotel. Its site isn't known but it doesn't appear to have been a great success and closed before the turn of the 20th century.

An invoice from the Rev A Leigh Harding of 3a Prospect Place, Park Lane, Barnstaple was issued on 23 July 1951. For clerical duties at Parracombe on eight Sundays during June and July that year he sought reimbursement of £3 3s per service, amounting to £25 4s in total. In addition he claimed for three single bus fares, each costing 1s 10d, making 5s 6d in total. On one occasion he took a car from Newport on account of a storm at a cost of 3s.

There was also a strong Methodist tradition in the village. In his memoirs Henry Blackmore (1868-1943) refers to his Uncle George Smyth, a follower of Wesleyan doctrine who lived at the bottom of the village when Blackmore was up at Court Place. In a manner which Henry describes as 'exceedingly quaint', George liked to dress in billowing trousers resembling pantaloons. Instead of shaking hands he would offer up his foot to be kissed whenever he greeted the young Blackmore.

Uncle George was also a philanthropist. He gave away free 'tickets' for meat and coal to the village poor and built the Wesleyan Chapel in 1839 at a cost of £100. He supported the chapel all his life and his daughter, Eliza, was Sunday School teacher there.

George's other claim to fame was that he and his wife Sophia (nee Blackmore, the youngest of ten children) possessed the only grape vine in the parish. It was their son Arthur who wrote the history of Parracombe, often quoted in this book, and who served as local correspondent for the North Devon Journal. From the limited records that survive we also know that the building was repaired in 1866, with two front windows fitted, at a total cost of £30.

According to a letter written by Reuben Blackmore in 1896 members of the chapel would sometimes preach in the open air around the village.

Molly Smyth, who was born at Higher Bodley in 1913 remembers attending Sunday School at the Wesleyan Chapel, an experience sometimes as entertaining as it was spiritual. 'Some of the bigger boys used to put red top matches on the top of the Tortoise Stove and watch them fire off,' she recalled. 'One of the match tops landed in the beard of the Sunday School teacher. We all watched horrified as a wisp of smoke curled up from his beard, expecting him to go up in flames like Moses and the burning

A Sunday School outing to Lee Bay in 1921.

bush. Fortunately, he didn't and carried on with his prayers unaware of the episode.

'I also went to Mrs McClennen's Bible class at Orchardside. Mrs McClennen was a very enthusiastic person and played the organ with great gusto. The main attraction of going to Bible class was that you were given an orange, a rare treat in those days.'

The first wedding to take place in the Wesleyan Chapel occurred almost 100 years after it was built. The bride was Elsie May Smyth, grand-daughter of the chapel builder, and Ernest Tucker.

The last service held in the Wesleyan Chapel took place in 1992, shortly before its sale. There was an outcry when the Chapel went on the market as some villagers were convinced that a child was buried beneath its floor. A memorial embedded in the church wall is dedicated to George Huxtable Smyth who died on 20th October 1848 at the age of three after an attack of croup. He was a son of George and Sophia and a brother of Arthur, although they are all buried elsewhere. In his history, Arthur points out that '...there is a monument to the memory of George Huxtable, son of George and Sophia Smyth, who died in 1848, the vault is on the left hand side of the aisle.'

In those days there was no shortage of religious outlets in Parracombe. Village draper Charles Blackmore (linked by marriage to the Smyths) founded a Plymouth Brethren chapel at his home, The Laurels, and a gospel hall also operating under Brethren principles was opened on the new bypass by Ada Blackmore (Henry's sister, born at Court Place) . Ada had returned to Parracombe after a spell as a missionary in China. She died in 1949, leaving a will valued at £386. Another brother, Josiah, went to Algiers as a missionary for 30 years before moving to the US, eventually taking a church post in Boston, Massachusetts. He returned to England during the Second World War to live in

8 School Report

'Attendances for past fortnight very low - cause sheep shearing'.

During the first decades of the 19th century education was something of a buzz word in Britain. Already Sunday schools were in vogue, following the initiative taken by Robert Raikes in 1780. Concerned about children hanging around in the streets, he began teaching reading and writing on Sundays in his home city of Gloucester for free, his conditions for admittance being that scholars washed their hands and faces and combed their hair. By 1795 an estimated 250,000 children around the country were going to Sunday school for education and eventually weekday lessons were offered in what were known as 'Ragged Schools'.

There were also two societies in existence to promote schooling. One was the British and Foreign School Society, supported by the Nonconformist churches; the other was the National Society for Promoting the Education of the Poor in the Principle of the Establish Church, backed by the Church of England. Teachers taught monitors and monitors educated pupils, keeping the costs down to 4s 2d per head per year. In addition, philanthropists provided some further schools.

We don't know what manner of schooling took place in Parracombe although there are some intriguing clues. The earliest mention of a school appears on an 1813 return issued by the Home Office, which states that 32 pupils were being taught here by Mr Charles Blackmore and Miss Grace Jones. It isn't clear, though, where the school was.

The following entry dated 3 April 1820 appears in the vestry minutes book 1813-1854.

'A publick vestry (*meeting of parishioners*) held at the Fox & Goose Inn in the Parish of Paracombe of which Publick Notice was given two Sundays previous to the meeting, to consult about giving two poor rates a year for supporting and promoting the Sunday school and for the weekly instruction of six poor children.'

Beneath are listed nine names, including David Lock Roach, James Smyth, Philip Tucker, John Lock Roach, Philip Dovell, William Lovering, William Lock and Richard Lovering.

Perhaps the most enlightening and astonishing information comes from a House of Commons inquiry document issued for the 1833 Education Act - which led to the government helping to finance education through the two church societies named above.

The document, although unsigned, appears to be in the hand of Rev John Pyke, longstanding Rector of Parracombe. The entries are untidy and it seems like a trial run before the real document is filled out and sent off. It was found in a box of items about Parracombe, alongside the vestry notes.

It reveals that there were 409 people in Parracombe on the population return of 1831. The entries indicate that four daily schools existed here in addition to two Sunday Schools. The first daily school had 30 pupils aged between two and ten years. The second, established in 1831, had 32 scholars aged between seven and 18. A third school with pupils from four to eighteen years dated from 1822 while the fourth, started in 1823, had ten pupils aged between four and 12. The first Sunday school

An early 20th century photograph of Parracombe school also giving a rare glimse of the cottage opposite - at one time occupied by Mr Polkinghorne the cobbler.

boasted no fewer than 64 pupils while the second had a creditable 34 in attendance.

In answer to a funding query, Pyke writes: 'The daily schools are supported by payments from the scholars. The Sunday school no 1 is supported by the Rector of the Parish, no 2 by the Sunday School Society.'

Hard though it is to believe, children in Parracombe had a choice of schools back then, even at nursery age.

The school we know today has existed on its present site since at least 1841. There's no wall plaque however to reveal a construction date. On 29th December 1881 the freehold of the school (amounting to 18 perches of land*) was donated by John Pyke Nott into the trust of Parracombe's minister, his churchwardens and their successors. The school managers on the trust deed are listed as the minister, churchwardens, Mr Pyke Nott of Bydown House, Swimbridge, and five other people.

Pyke Knott's ancestors are buried in an altar tomb surrounded by iron railings at St Petrock's, although there's no record of him or his grave at the site. The tomb includes the remains of John Pyke, rector and patron at Parracombe for 42 years before his death in 1868. He was married to Elizabeth Nott, of Bydown House, Swimbridge. The west side of the tomb bears the family coat of arms.

In 1883 the school roll was at its largest, with 89 pupils registered. The lowest number recorded

** A perch is equivalent to five and a half yards or, squared, is thirty and a quarter square yards.*

during the 20th century was 36 - in 1941, 1946 and 1967. Parents paid for their children's education until 1891 when fees were finally abolished.

The school log reveals that an early schoolroom was enlarged to its present size early in 1875, at a cost of £30, with the intention of accommodating 60 children. Facilities were primitive. Children had to take drinking water from the same stream that their urine and excrement was discharged into and it wasn't until the Rural Sanitary Authority intervened (some time after 1890) that the girls' closet at the school was equipped with a pail.

In 1884 the school's thatched roof was replaced with slate, although it wasn't until 1905 that the main room was given a new window and a water supply installed. During this era inspectors' reports referred to the school as inadequate, damp, unsatisfactory and uncared for. Records indicate that it was flooded in 1900, 1905, 1906, 1909 and in 1918 while in 1945, 1947 and 1963 it was closed because of heavy snow. In January 1907 the classroom was so cold that ink froze in the inkwells and it wasn't until 1954, the year the school canteen was added, that electricity was installed. Even then, it was 1977 before night storage heaters replaced the solid fuel stoves.

By 1912 the playground was properly surfaced, making it safer, although by November 1928 it was necessary to raise further funds (including £7 from a school concert) to effect repairs. By then the state of the playing area was so bad that physical training frequently had to be abandoned. The existing infants' room was added in 1927 and the following year the Board of Education permitted the school to house 77 pupils. In 1942 pupil numbers rose significantly when Martinhoe School was closed down

In February 1873 the entire community was stunned by the death of schoolmaster John Lock after he froze to death trying to walk home in a snowstorm. The tragedy was reported as follows in a local newspaper:

'Mr John Lock, aged 49, schoolmaster of this place and registrar of births, deaths and marriages for the district, came to a very melancholy end on Saturday night last, having perished in a snow storm within little more than half a mile from his own house. Deceased had been in at Barnstaple to deliver his registers and to settle a little account with the Superintendant registrar which he did early in the afternoon and, having transacted some other business, set out to walk home - a distance of 12 miles - before evening.

'A fall of snow came on, but it was not heavy until the evening had far advanced. Deceased was seen at Loxhore about half way between Barnstaple and his home, and was left by a person in the road, saying that he should soon get home. Poor fellow! The hope deceived him. He never reached home but was found next morning in a snow drift in a lane out of the main road between Blackmoor Gate and Parracombe quite dead and frozen!'

The man who found him - and presumably wrote the above item - was none other than our old friend, historian and newspaper correspondent, Arthur Smyth.

Secret marriage

Two years later scandal enveloped the school when its head teacher, Elizabeth Thomas, secretly married. She gave in her notice but was forced to leave immediately after the Rector discovered that the clandestine wedding had taken place at 'a Dissenting Chapel in Barnstaple'. He considered her conduct 'reprehensible' and prematurely shut the school. This closure occurred on 20th August, implying there were no lengthy summer holidays at the time.

Miss Thomas's replacement was a temporary one, 20-year-old Sarah Gould, from Barnstaple. From 1876 the job was held by Eliza Rawle - who became Mrs Crocombe after her marriage three years later. Before she left in 1882 the original infant classroom had been added, with room for a further 21 children.

An enduring problem for all teachers at Parracombe was the high rate of absenteeism among pupils - well above that of similar schools in the area.

In 1881 following an official inspection it was reported that 'the managers do not appear to be aware of the existence of (attendance) bye laws'.

After she left Mrs Crocombe started a 'Private Adventure School' locally which reduced the pupil roll at Parracombe during the three years it ran. One of the first actions of her successor, Alfred Brown, had been to issue demands to parents for the payment of school fees and arrears. Brown's concern about the pattern of absences is also evident from the school log. On 5th July 1884 he noted: 'Attendances for past fortnight very low - cause sheep shearing'.

When the attendance dipped as low as 33 in August 1886 he wrote: 'This is partly due to sickness, hay carrying, wet day and carelessness of parents'. Three days afterwards he observed that more than 50 per cent of his pupils were absent. 'Of these 24 per cent are sick, eight per cent at work harvesting, 17 per cent at home work (baby minding, mothers at Lynton with market stuff)'. In September 1886 he wrote: 'Fifty per cent of boys away assisting at corn harvest'. Two years later he again had a pop at parents observing that the 'Attendance Officer still continues to serve notices on some parents but the familiarity breeds contempt.'

Brown taught reading, writing, arithmetic, spelling and scripture. He was obviously not a popular man and in 1885 his professional skills were questioned in an inspector's report which referred to 'an air of torpor *[which]* pervades the whole school'. Three years later another report highlighted 'a lack of animation in the teaching'. Despite this classes were occasionally brought to life, such as when Edison's phonograph was shown to excited pupils in 1895.

Brown stayed until 1898 when he took up a post at Berrynarbor School. His departure may have been inspired by a crisis at the school reported in the Journal on 29th March 1898:

'The Rector informed us at the Parish Meeting that school matters were not very flourishing financially and that unless the attendance of the children increased it would be impossible to continue as at present - in short we must either reduce expenses or increase the rate. Some advocate a return to the old system of a mistress, which would be less expensive and equally effective. Some 15 years ago we had a most efficient mistress and the attendance was 70-80. She had two monitors for some time. When they retired she asked for an assistant. Being refused she resigned. Now with an attendance of 30 to 40 there is a master and infant mistress, the fact being that as attendance has decreased expenses have increased.'

Brown's departure was unlikely to have been greeted with dismay among pupils who surely lived in fear of the cane. When Brown punished one boy for bullying the father of the child took out a summons against him for assault. However the case was abandoned when the parent failed to appear at court in Lynton.

Despite his reputation as a disciplinarian, and shortcomings as a teacher, Brown was not without his supporters. In 1954 a correspondent to the local paper wrote: 'He certainly didn't believe in sparing the rod, not on me anyway, but when I left to complete my education in London I was able to look back with respect and affection on many things that he had taught me.

'This year I visited the new churchyard and saw his grave and, although I have travelled far and wide over the world and seen many wonderful things, I felt sincerely that I owed a great debt of gratitude to this simple man, so long Parracombe's teacher. When I left the village there was no one buried in the new churchyard (I believe Mr Davy was the first in 1894) but now the Reaper has been very busy and many of my old schoolmates and relations lie there.' The writer's initials were FJS.

FJS's sentiments were clearly shared by the school's managers. In 1899, the year after Brown left, they arranged a presentation in the form of a framed, illuminated testimonial (done in oils by one Mr W L

Baron, an art teacher in Barnstaple) and a purse of money. The language was surprisingly respectful and affectionate.

Dear Mr Brown
For over sixteen years you have been master of our parochial school and the excellent reports of the Inspectors show that your work has been very successful.

After so long and close a connexion it is felt that you should not be allowed to leave without some token of our regard and goodwill.

We therefore ask you to kindly accept the purse and its contents, which we beg to hand you herewith on behalf of the following subscribers. [62 names are listed].

'We trust that in the important post of Master of the Berrynarbor School to which you have been appointed you may be equally successful as here and that every prosperity may attend you to the end of your career.

We remain yours, very trully
John Smyth
William Lock
George Court
R S Allison: committee

Brown's replacement was William Durrant Bunn, who retired in 1904 without apparently remedying the school's shortcomings. An inspectors report in 1902 points out that 'methods are of a mechanical nature and not likely to develop the general intelligence of the children'.

Bunn worked alongside his sister Emma and they received a joint salary of £100. In 1905 headmaster Cyril Davis had an annual income of £90 while his assistant, Ethel Blackmore, who began work at the school in August that year, received just £8. By 1911 the headmaster was John Burden, on £88 a year, and Miss Blackmore had leapt up the pay scale to earn a £30 salary as the senior of two assistants. Burden had Evenlode, the house next to the school, built.

A report by the Exeter Diocesan Inspector of Schools dated 3rd May 1907 reveals that there were 64 pupils in the school. Some reservations were expressed about the depth of religious education although the report ends with the observation that work had been interrupted 'to a large extent owing to a serious outbreak of mumps'. Diocesan inspections, during which knowledge of the catechism and prayer book was supposed to be demonstrated by pupils, continued for many years.

More discipline

The school was also regularly inspected by the local education authority. Following a visit on 24th August 1910 an inspector wrote: 'Progress has been hindered by frequent changes in the teaching staff. The instruction is planned on sound lines and the children show a reasonable amount of knowledge and intelligence. The present head teacher has effected improvement in many respects, but the discipline needs attention and the written work should be neater.'

In 1917 there were 41 pupils on the books, comprising 18 infants, 17 juniors and six senior pupils. Ethel Blackmore was teaching the infants while John Burden taught the rest. Ethel was the daughter of Charles Blackmore and his second wife Elizabeth Stenner who lived at Court Place in Churchtown. Apart from two years at college in Exeter obtaining teaching qualifications, she spent her entire life in Parracombe and was still teaching in 1954.

An article in the *Picture Post* about Parracombe (dated 3rd July 1954 and mentioned in Chapter Two) revealed that: '[Miss Blackmore] has spent all but two of the last 60 years in the village school as pupil, monitoress and teacher. Since 1925 she hasn't missed half-a-day.' Ethel lived with her sister Christine at Meadowdene, two doors from the school, and is buried at the old church.

The most promising pupils were recommended for tuition at Barnstaple Grammar School and in June 1921 Parracombe's head received the following letter

Miss Blackmore teaching in the junior classroom in 1954.

from the clerk to the governors there: 'The little girl Berry you entered for the Scholarship Examination did not get into the list of Free Places but she might possibly be recommended for an extra place if the parents could afford to keep her here all the week as it would be useless trying to come in daily.' In 1934 headmistress Miss Blackmore decided two pupils, Mary Hancock and Ernest Jenkins, were sufficiently able to compete for a free place in the scholarship exams. According to her report 'their parents were notified to that effect but neither sat for the examination'. Sadly, even the brightest pupils at Parracombe had limited opportunities.

Thanks to records kept at the school we have an indication of the punishments meted out over two decades, beginning in 1925. In that year Ernest Blackmore was given two strokes for 'deliberately injuring his sister by rough play in the playground'. The following year William Dallyn received three strokes for 'poor conduct'. On 20th May 1942 William Delbridge was given one stroke for 'disturbing the class'. A single stroke was the punishment most commonly administered and there are no instances of more than three strokes being given. The misdemeanors that most often occurred were disobedience, throwing stones and rudeness.

Bill Delbridge remembers: 'I didn't used to get on so well with Miss Blackmore and I used to get the cane quite a lot. I'm not sure if it was a cane or a ruler but it hurt. It was across the top of the fingers where you get more pain, rather than the palm.

'We used to come home for dinner. Miss Blackmore had a great bell that she would ring at the end of dinner time.'

As a child he walked and cycled for miles, getting to know every gully and combe in the area. 'Very

The Worth family who moved from Lundy Island to Parracombe in 1923. Back row: Fred, Bill and Annie (York). Front row: Edie and Emma.

often you went out on your own. I was alone when I shot myself in the finger at the quarry while I was out shooting rabbits.

'I left school at 14 and worked at a nursery in Lynton. There wasn't any employment in Parracombe. Then I had national service, which was the best thing I ever did. I joined the medical corps and went to Egypt on a troop ship.' Afterwards he continued medical training and qualified before returning to the village to bring up a family.

Teaching equipment stored at the school in March 1925 included 56 inkwells, six crochet hooks, 20 pairs of wooden knitting needles and 42 sets of steel knitting needles, five dozen thimbles, one rope for jumping, one bat, six scholars' blackboards and eight boxes of counters. Twenty seven years later the range of recorded stock was only marginally improved. Records list four crochet hooks, 42 sets of steel knitting needles, two whistles for the school yard, one magnifying glass, one clock face, seven boxes of hardwood building bricks, eight set squares, one compass, one football, seven ropes for jumping, 28 for skipping and a total of 29 hoops.

In 1925 Annie York, now of Peel House, joined the school as a pupil after her family moved to Parracombe from Lundy Island. Her clearest memories are of knitting and sewing lessons. 'I used to make aprons, little aprons with a frill around the bib,' she said.

'Miss Blackmore was my teacher. She was the only teacher in the big room. We used to get an attendance officer come to visit if you stayed away. He used to come to your home to find the reason why.

'We were allowed out into the roads at lunchtime. We played hare and hounds across the fields. We walked to school from Brakebrook.'

Annie left school aged 14 and then worked at Shirwell as housemaid to the Rev Charles Chichester, father of round-the-world sailor Sir Francis. 'I came home on half days,' she recalled. 'I would cycle to Chelfham station and put the bike either on the train or leave it at the station, and get the train to Parracombe Halt. It broke my heart the first time I came home. I was a bit homesick, but I stayed at Shirwell for two years.'

William Delbridge senior went to Parracombe School in 1905 and was taught by Mr Burden, who at that time lived in The Terrace. He left on his 14th birthday in the same year that World War 1 began. Before Mr Delbridge's death he recalled the coal stove which heated the school and the paraffin lights occasionally used to brighten up the classrooms, during a taped interview with Parracombe schoolchildren.

When he left to join his father's horse-drawn haulier business Mr Delbridge was a flute player in the village's pipe and drum band. He also played in the brass band before it was wound up.

When George Smyth was at school between 1915 and 1925 he was forced to use a pen in his right hand when he was naturally left-handed. In a taped interview he remembered the inkwells in the desks into which pens were frequently dipped. His most treasured memory of school was a regular outing by

Miss Blackmore taking the children for country dancing with the aid of a wind-up gramophone, circa 1950.

horse and cart to Lee Bay or Woody Bay. Two other boys on the school register shared his name.

Reports by the headmistress Miss Blackmore give a remarkable insight into school life in the 1930s when there were prefects and three different 'houses'. 'In July 1929 the School Doctor forbade William George and John Crocombe to use ordinary school books or to follow the usual course of study until they were provided with suitable glasses,' she notes. 'Owing to his instructions these children have been debarred from practically all lessons except oral ones. They have made a very little progress in speech but their position is far from satisfactory.

'HMI Miss Cooke inspected the school in September. Unfortunately some of the brighter children were absent owing to Barnstaple Fair, but that fact did not prevent her from spending the whole day in the school.' We learn that Ruby Latham (who became Mrs Court) won the essay competition that year, writing about 'Kindness to Animals' and winning herself a copy of Kipling's *Jungle Tales*. She went on to secure a free place at Barnstaple Grammar School. Christine Newton won a prize for the best darning among the girls.

In 1932 country dancing was introduced to the curriculum (with the help of seven records and a

The Dairy Class outside the RAOB Hall. Back row: Audrey Smyth, Margery Smyth, Henry Harding, Jack Edwards, Walter Nicholls, Ernie Davey, Dorothy Land and an unknown instructor. Middle row: Winnie Trump. Molly Crocombe, Rita Parkhouse, Dulcie Court, Georgina Tucker, Reenie Oatway, Daisy Nicholls, Doreen Tucker and Mary Hancock. Front row: Bess Davey, unknown, instructor, Bertha Harris, instructor, Betty Smyth, Mrs C Land and Nancy Driscoll.

gramophone) and a small display was given 'in the town hall at the request of the women's institute committee'. In the same year senior girls from Parracombe went to cookery classes in Barnstaple once a week while senior boys were taught basketry.

A progress report dated 31st March 1934 reveals the pupils took tests that month in scripture, reading, poetry, composition, literature, spelling, penmanship, geography, history, arithmetic, nature study, hygiene, handiwork, drawing, needlework and physical training. 'Frederick Creek won the highest total marks - 84-5 per cent - thereby receiving a savings certificate as a reward.'

In the mid 1930s pupils attended butter-making classes held at the Buff Hall during school hours. Among the pupils at this time was Marjorie Bray (nee Smyth) who remembers turning up to school wearing a simple apron and the boys and girls using different playgrounds. Her most enduring memory of school is the sewing tuition she received. 'I still make my own clothes now and I have never had any other lessons.'

Shortly after she left school she joined her sister in Bickington to cultivate land for the war effort, returning to Parracombe by bus every weekend.

Audrey Petherick was at Parracombe School between 1928 and 1937 and her childhood memories prove why dairy classes were so relevant. 'After school I used to have to fetch the cows in for milking. I was "helped" in this job by our retired sheep dog Rover who would be patiently waiting for me to come home from school. I wasn't allowed to take the young dog Carlo, as he would chase the cows and swing on their tails and he didn't do anything I told him.

'While I was changing into my old clothes and eating a piece of cake, Rover would be rushing in and out of the kitchen barking his head off. Mother would say "hurry up maid and vetch the cows, that dug is driving me maze". Rover didn't have the slightest

The Parracombe School photo of 1932. Back Row: John Beard, Jack Edwards, Claude Harris, Dorothy Hoyles, Edith Worth, Beryl Bevan, Margaret Harris, Francis Poole, Fred Creek, Ken de Lancey. Middle Row: Ernest Davey, William Nicholls, John Barrow, Ena Ridd, Emma Worth, Molly Crocombe, Audrey Smyth, Mary Hancock, John Crocombe, Frank Edwards, William Tucker. Seated: Gladys Leworthy, Muriel Barrow, Joy de Lancey, Lorna Delbridge, Amy Tucker, Kathleen Beard, Audrey Shapland, ? Land, ? Land, Doreen Tucker, Joyce Saders, Daisy Nicholls
Reg Tucker, Henry Harding, Ken Barrow, Herbert Crocombe, Cecil Tossell, William Land, Roy Worth, Kelvin Crocombe, Monty Leworthy, Stanley Sanders, Ernest Pickard. Teachers: - Miss Larkcombe and Miss Ethel Blackmore

interest in the cows, all he minded was sniffing everying gatepost and vuzz bush in sight. He did give a token bark now and again but anyway, the cows knew what they had to do without any help from Rover or me.'

Shortly before the outbreak of the Second World War pupils were provided with Horlick's Malted Milk at break time. However, its health-giving properties were insufficient to prevent an influenza epidemic in the spring of 1939 which kept more than threequarters of pupils away from school.

After 1946 senior pupils were transferred to Combe Martin Secondary School. In that year there were just 36 children aged five to eleven left at Parracombe but, according to a Ministry of Education inspectors' report dated 28th May 1946, the reorganisation had led to younger children thriving 'under the fine influence of an experienced and capable Head Mistress supported by a loyal and painstaking assistant'. The report praises the school as a 'lively and happy little community, wherein teachers and scholars alike are making an effective contribution.'

However it goes on to criticise the accommodation. 'There are only two rooms, each of which is in the occupation of a class, with the result that there is no free space within the building for activities or for dining...the playground is unsatisfactory, having a steep fall and a rough surface.' The inspectors conclude: 'Altogether it is clear that this little school is making good use of its rather restricted opportunities.'

Criticism of the school's cramped accommodation was a regular theme for inspectors, teachers, parents and governors in later decades. It wasn't until the spring of 2004, after a protracted ten-year campaign, that the school finally gained a new classroom at a cost of around £100,000.

9 High Days and Holidays

Let's wake 'em up a little bit, let's stir 'em up a little bit, come on Parracombe - 'tis Revelling time!

The Revels, a spring festival celebrated at Whitsun, has long been a key date on the village's social calendar. Its roots are uncertain although Arthur Smyth's history of 1876 sketches the following picture:

'A Revel is held on White Sunday (as it is called) and Whitmonday at which, years ago, there was a good deal of drunkenness and hilarity. The public houses would get little brass tea-kettles and the like to be played for at skittles. This ancient custom was continued until quite recent years. There is nothing doing here now although Spurrier takes his stand for lollipops etc on Whitmondays and some of the children will congregate and buy a few things from him. Like the rest of the village customs the Revels are now a thing that was and used to be.

'Half a century ago wrestling matches took place at the Revels. Young men would strip above the waist to leave nothing but bare skin for their opponents to catch hold of. I have *[heard]* an old prize wrestler say that when he and his brother used to practice for amusement their bodies would be covered with blood where they had dug their nails into each other.'

A newspaper report dated 31st May 1898 adds to the scene. ' Some say it is the anniversary of the dedication of the Church, rather a singular explanation as the revel certainly possessed little that was reverent. Wrestling matches, the skittle alley and the public house were well patronised. The person having the arrangement of the games attended church with spoons stuck in his hat band and at the close of the service mounted the nearest tombstone and read the programme for the morrow's amusements with the various prizes. During the Sunday evening sweets, nuts and gingerbreads were retailed through the village.'

The anniversary service held by the Wesleyan Sunday School superseded the ancient Revel and its festivities. There were morning and evening services on the Sunday, with singing by the schoolchildren during the afternoon. On Monday afternoon at Halwell Barton between two and four o'clock the children played games and were rewarded by nuts and sweets. There was tea at the town hall before the games resumed.

Henry Blackmore (of Court Place, rather than the distantly related Henry Blackmore at the Fox & Goose) recalls the occasion held on the first Sunday of June. 'This was a red letter both for farmers and scholars when we were called upon to recite pieces and sing special choruses etc for which we had a months practise. This was by a tea on Monday sports in a field lent by Mr Gammin and meeting in the evening when some more pieces were recited and special singing given.'

In the last half of the 19th century the Wesleyan Chapel also organised annual outings by hay cart to Lynmouth or beyond. According to Henry Blackmore 'we had a good ramble, a grand feed and a round of games'.

Revels was reinstated in 1954 when the first queen was Angela Kift, attended by Mary Court and Sylvia Crang. They were chosen in a ballot of school pupils. The page boys were Michael Richards and

Stephen Petherick. Alas, bad weather meant many of the planned events had to be cancelled or curtailed.

The following song was penned for the occasion by Dick Turpin, a driving force behind the new Revels and proprietor of Parracombe's local garage, which then traded at Blackmoor Gate.

'Come let's be merry, let's be merry,
Come let us sing all you girls and lads,
Come let's be merry, let's be merry,
Join in a song all you mums and dads.
For since all Parracombe has gone mad,
Why should the rest of Devon be sad.
Let's wake 'em up a little bit,
Let's stir 'em up a little bit,
Come on Parracombe - 'tis Revelling time!

Let not tomorrow bring you sorrow,
While the stream of life flows on,
Let not tomorrow bring you sorrow,
Darkest hours are quickly gone.
For when this happy day is done,
There will still be time for fun,
Whatever troubles life may bring,
You'll feel much better if you sing,
Come on Parracombe - 'tis Revelling time!

Notes from 1955 reveal the committee that year comprised a representative from the British Legion, Buffs, Rifle Club, Parish Council, Women's Institute and school. Others were elected or co-opted on to the committee, including the wife of the Hon James Lindsay (the local MP who lived at Heddon Hall). The chair was the Rev. John Lynn (in post from 1951-1957), vice chair was Dick Turpin and the secretary and treasurer was Fred Sanders. Pam Latham was crowned Revels queen that year by Mr Lindsay. Her attendants were Sylvia Crang and Barbara White while the page boys were Freddie Sanders and Brian Dallyn.

In his report Mr Sanders talks about the opening of the skittle alley (constructed with proceeds from the 1954 Revels) opposite the Fox & Goose. Built by W. H. Lethaby, the building was officially opened on 16th October 1954 by the local MP Mr Lindsay and was apparently used during both summer and winter.

Buoyed by the triumph of the celebrations, Mr Sanders had great expectations for the future. 'While the past Revels have been successful, we must plan for bigger and better events in the future,' he wrote. 'Once you have set a high standard it is up to the committee to maintain that standard. I also feel that there is a strong case both for and against having more side shows and decorated vehicles in the carnival procession.'

In the past villagers also took full advantage of national celebrations. Queen Victoria's Jubilee in 1887 provided an excellent excuse for a village party and we know that Polly Court, aged 11, collected cash door to door. This event was partly financed by an earlier concert, details of which are unknown. One newspaper report of an unspecified royal occasion - probably the wedding of the future Edward VII - illustrates the length to which locals would go in pursuit of a good time:

'A very long and gay procession started from the school, headed by the Parracombe Brass Band and

The official openng of the skittle alley in 1954 with the first ball bowled by local MP Mr Lindsay - apparently formal dress was not required.

Parracombe Brass Band photographed outside The Rectory (Heddon Hall). The bass drum is stiull in use on Revel Day.
1 Bill Leworthy (drowned in flood)
2 Parson Chanter
3 Tom Barrow
4 Bill Tamlyn
5 Curate Leakey

consisting of school children with flags, mounted Foresters, members of the Order, Juvenile Foresters, members of Good Fellowship Society, all in full regalia; committee, each wearing a commemorative medal. Flags were freely displayed along the line of route and the Union Jack Van was gay with bunting. At 3 pm the children had tea, followed by a dinner of bread, beef and beer for men and a tea for the women.

'A capital programme of athletic sports was then carried out. Sir H P Carew acted as starter and Rev Chanter and Mr C V Wilks were judges. Dancing to the strains of the band, which played most creditably, kiss-in-the-ring etc filled up the time. About 10 a huge bonfire was lit on the top of Holwell Castle and as it died away there was a most magnificent display of fireworks from Brock's, generously provided by Sir Henry Carew. These were managed by Rev J F Chanter and were immensely enjoyed. Three hearty cheers were given for Sir Henry, Rev J F Chanter and Mr Wilks and about midnight closed a day's proceedings, the most enjoyable and pleasant ever seen in this parish.'

Early in 1900 the School Log shows that Parracombe children were given an afternoon off to celebrate the relief of Ladysmith, a town in South Africa which had been under siege by the Boers for 118 days. 'The children assembled and sang God Save the Queen and cheered the generals and their men,' according to the entry. A further holiday was instituted to mark the end of the Boer War.

Saints v sinners

It's tempting to imagine the village pulling together to organise local functions with lots of back-slapping and good-humour but it wasn't always so. Plans to

Coronation celebrations, 1953.

mark the coronation of Edward VII, one time visitor to Parracombe, caused quite a stir in Parracombe with organisers separating into two factions. A letter from a parishioner published in the North Devon Journal on 7th July 1902 explains:

'Stories have gone forth to the effect that there has been a considerable amount of unpleasantness here over the Coronation festivities. This is most erroneous. The real fact was that there were too many placed on the committee.'In the multitude of councillors there is wisdom' but the difficulty amongst so many was that they couldn't decide who possessed the greatest wisdom and as they could not agree they agreed to differ and by a singular coincidence the natives went together, while those who had come into the parish more recently went with the Parson and were facetiously known as the saints and sinners. They may have been a few hot words spoken during the heat of debate as is very frequently the case.

'Of course, as reported, there were two celebrations, both very similar. The sinners were to have a bonfire and sheep shearing extra. The saints held their concert; the sinners apparently could not sing and for music they had the village brass band. Curiously enough half the parish appear to be sinners the other half are saints, at any rate they were pretty evenly distributed although the sinners had more visitors. All passed off splendidly on both sides and now all is over we are all friends again as neighbours should be and we all unite in the hope that the King's health may be soon restored.'

To mark the Queen's coronation on 2nd June 1953 there was a service in the Parish Church conducted by the Rector, the Rev. John Lynn, and the Methodist minister, the Rev. W Palmer Morris.

Afterwards there were children's sports on the recreation ground, organised by teacher Ethel Blackmore, and later members of the Women's Institute prepared a public tea at the Buff Hall.

At 7.30 pm there was a grand carnival procession from Churchtown to the Fox & Goose with prizes for the best-decorated car, tractor, horse-drawn vehicle and bike. Awards were also given for the prettiest, most original and most comical fancy dress with a special section for horse and pony riders.

When it was over all the children were presented with a souvenir spoon, paid for by Mr H Petherick and Mr H Harding, and a New Testament donated by Mr B C Tucker. The day ended with a dance at the Buff Hall organised by the local branch of the British Legion and a bonfire on Holworthy Ridge, run by Bill Hagley and members of the Rifle Club.

PARRACOMBE REVEL
SILVER JUBILEE
1953 - 1978

SOUVENIR
PROGRAMME

On 7th June 1977 Parracombe marked the Queen's silver jubilee with a lunch for the senior village folk followed by a football match in which men had to dress as women and everyone wore wellies. There was a special prize for the most feminine male. Then there were games and competitions, including a pillow fight and a wheelbarrow race, and the presentation of Jubilee beakers by Revels chairman Harry Latham. From here the focus moved to a Jubilee tea at the Buff Hall and a fancy dress competition for the under 11s, with costumes made from crepe paper only. A social gathering went on well into the evening.

Clay pigeon shooting at The Revels. Freddie Leworthy shooting with Fred Rawle kneeling at the trap.

Newspaper reports occasionally offer valuable insights into family events, such as this account of a Parracombe wedding celebration:

'On 10th May 1893 the marriage of John Rottenbury and Fanny Wood, daughter of Mr F Wood of Hillside Cottage. A subscription had been opened at the Fox and Goose, with friends pledging money for Rottenbury. A total of £7 14 shillings was raised to buy gifts. The following framed testimonial was presented to the couple on their wedding day. 'This testimonial together with a handsome dinner service

PROGRAMME OF EVENTS

SATURDAY, 27th MAY — RAOB HALL

7.30 p.m. Crowning of Revel Queen
Miss Julie Leworthy

Attendants: Jill Petherick & Linda Puttick

Pages: Dean Roy & Daniel Ford

8.00 p.m. Concert with local artists and guests.

SUNDAY, 28th MAY — ST PETROCK'S CHURCH

3.00 p.m.. Revel Jubilee Service.

MONDAY, 29th MAY — PLAYING FIELD

1.30 p.m. Fancy Dress and Float Judging
By Westward T.V. Star, Gus Honeybun
with Miss E. van den Berghe

2.00 p.m. Procession around village.
Barnstaple British Legion Town Band.

3.00 p.m. Races, Side Shows, Tug-o-War, etc.

9.00 p.m. - 1 a.m. RAOB HALL
Dancing to Savana 3.

PARRACOMBE REVEL SONG

On Revel Day in Parracombe,
We sing this merry song,
And very soon you'll know the tune,
And sing it all day long,
Though every word is quite absurd,
And some will hardly rhyme,
On Revel Day in Parracombe / We have a proper time.

On Revel Day in Parracombe,
We set all cares aside,
If jobs aren't done or not begun,
We simply let 'em bide,
We sing and play from break of day,
Until the midnight chime,
On Revel Day in Parracome / We have a proper time.

On Revel Day in Parracombe,
We eat and drink our fill,
And make a feast for man and beast,
Of kindness and goodwill,
No wicked word is ever heard,
There's no such thing as crime,
On Revel Day in Parracome / We have a proper time.

On Revel Day in Parracombe,
The band plays loud and long,
And every man, as best he can,
Joins in this jolly song,
Though some may scoff, we are not put off,
We think it sounds sublime!!
On Revel Day in Parracome / We have a proper time.

The programme for the Revel Silver Jubilee of 1978 - showing the Revel song as it now sung. Revels was re-introduced in 1954 following a highly successful Coronation celebration the previous year.

of Doulton ware, a tea service, a bedstead with spring mattress etc complete was presented to Mr John Rottenbury R S S on the occasion of his marriage 10th May 1893 from a large number of his friends in the parish and neighbourhood who wish to show their esteem for him and desire for his future happiness and welfare.' A floral arch over 20 ft high was constructed and a volley of anvils saluted the happy couple as they left for their honeymoon.'

The papers were also peppered with reports of countryside sports. 'On 4th January 1865 a ploughing match was held on East Bodley Farm, Parracombe, the property of Mr William Lock, in three fields called Newberys. 'In the class of local man over 18 yrs of age 1st prize of £2 went to James Tamlyn, ploughman to N Snow esq of Parracombe, 2nd prize £1 5s to William Palmer ploughman to W Halliday of Glenthorne, 3rd prize 15s Jas Lewis, ploughman to Mr R D Blackmore of Arlington.'

In a similar era Henry Blackmore of the Fox and Goose Hotel held his first pigeon shooting match. The prizes were £5, £3 and £2. James Crocombe of Lynton came first, killing all his birds, while four runners up split the rest of the prize money having bagged seven a piece.

Both Ilfracombe Harriers and Barnstaple and

The Youth Club circa 1980 at the Revels Concert performing 'Death in Parracombe'. During the performance all the cast bar one died horribly on stage. James Tucker, playing the policeman, was unable to solve the riddle before even he too died.

North Devon Harriers met at the Fox & Goose on a regular basis. Coursing with greyhounds also took place on Parracombe Common and Chapman Barrows.

Parracombe even had its own horseracing track - above the junction at Parracombe Lane Head in fields bordering the left hand side of the road just before the Pleasure Ground. Sadly we haven't so far been able to trace any form guides or results.

Hunting and Parracombe

The cry of hounds and the sound of the horn have for generations resounded within the parish boundary of Parracombe. The Devon & Somerset Staghounds, Exmoor Foxhounds and North Devon Beagles, the three packs which regularly hunt the area, continue to produce fine hunts from this western end of the moor. The staghounds, which hunt the wild red deer, have not met within the village itself within living memory, but they do meet close by at Blackmoor Gate auction field on a regular basis both for autumn and spring staghunting. This remains a most popular fixture for mounted and motorised followers alike when, invariably, a stag is to be found within the Highley or Holworthy coverts.

Following the meet at Blackmoor Gate on 23 September 1989, when fog on the high ground looked threatening, the 'tufters' - experienced hounds - were let go on a stag at Twineford, just above the Parracombe by-pass. They ran well up the valley, crossed out on to Highley Combe and went out at the top of Homer Common to pass the Longstone just as the fog lifted miraculously. With hounds at full speed the line was straight over Cheriton Ridge and Farley Water towards Dry Bridges, crossed both the Brendon road and, with the pack now on, the Aldermans Barrow road and on to Blagdon Wood and down Snowdrop Valley (Wheddon Cross) to the Sawmills where the end came at 3.20pm. The report for that day concluded, 'This great hunt, with a point of 16 miles, was undoubtedly one of the best of recent times: an

unbeatable line in lovely still weather, with the going perfect. It will certainly be one for the history books'.

Mr Dick Lloyd, president of the Devon & Somerset Staghounds, recalls the autumn of 1952 when following the Barnstaple Fair meet, traditionally held at Yarde Down in September but on this occasion a month later due to the great flood, a stag was found quite late on in Beara Wood (Brayford) with a conclusion at a late hour at Cowley Wood. After a most welcome drink at Blackmoor Gate, for riders and horses alike, Dick Lloyd, together with fellow hunters, hacked home and on what had been a particularly dark day hurricane lanterns lit many of the bridges, which had been savagely mauled by the storms.

The Exmoor Foxhounds, established by Squire Nicholas Snow of Oare as 'the Stars of the West' in 1869, have hunted the Parracombe coverts since their inception and few seasons pass without a meet at Holworthy Farm, Killington Cross and Homer Common Gate with the Boxing Day meet being hosted by the proprietors of the Old Station Inn at Blackmoor Gate.

Meets at The Fox & Goose, Heddon Hall and East Bodley.

The 'Journal' reported C1890, 'The Exmoor hounds had a fine run, but while crossing Highley the fox was shot by someone, much to the annoyance of the field. The event has created considerable surprise as it is without precedent here. These hounds are extremely popular in this district, and the utmost harmony prevails between the worthy master and the farmers'. The 1893 opening meet of the Exmoor Foxhounds for the Parracombe district took place in September when, it is reported, 'the assembly of lovers of the chase was numerous and included Messrs Dallyn, Huxtable, Ridd, Sanders and Smyth', all names that are still familiar in the locality.

In the present day the North Devon Beagles and their supporters gather in the vicinity on a regular basis during the season with meets at Holworthy, East Bodley, Ladywell, Pleasure Ground and Homer Common Gate, while a century ago it was the Ilfracombe Harriers who enjoyed great sport hunting the brown hare.

In recent times a number of celebration meets have been held within the parish. On Saturday 26 November, 1988 the Exmoor Foxhounds met at Lorna Doone in celebration of Mr Harry Latham's 80th birthday. It was an immensely proud 'Mr Harry' who, alongside the master Captain Ronnie Wallace, led the mounted field to the moor for a day foxhunting. Saturday 4 February 1999 saw the Exmoor Foxhounds at Brimble View in honour of Mr Claude Rogers' 70th birthday and following his family's splendid hospitality to allcomers Claude, mounted on his black mare Katie, escorted the assembled field away from the meet to celebrate his birthday in style. Perhaps the most memorable birthday celebration is the mini hunting festival that was staged at Holworthy to mark Mr Dave Rawle's 80th birthday. The Devon & Somerset Staghounds accorded Dave and his family the greatest honour when, breaking with longstanding tradition, they met at Holworthy on Barnstaple Fair Saturday, 16 September 1995. Following generous hospitality for mounted and footfollowers alike, the Rawle family were to repeat the performance, not once but twice, just two days later when, on Dave's birthday, both the Exmoor Foxhounds and the North Devon Beagles met at the farm.

10 Parracombe at War

He survived some of the heaviest fighting of the war and during the height of battle on 18th August was promoted twice on the same day, first to corporal; then sergeant, reflecting the massive losses...

Usually, Parracombe's young men went into farming and its associated trades. However, school records and the village war memorial reveal that a substantial number also served in the armed forces, as volunteers or conscripts.

From 1782 the regiment of choice locally was the 11th (North Devonshire) Regiment of Foot - motto: *One And All*. A century later it became the Devonshire Regiment, dubbed 'The Bloody Eleventh' after suffering horrendous losses at the hands of Napoleonic forces during the 1812 Battle of Salamanca. It survived as a separate infantry force until 1958 when it was amalgamated with another to form the Devonshire and Dorset Regiment.

Men from the Bloody Eleventh served in Australia between 1845 and 1857, when it was still a penal colony. Although they were comparatively well paid they served in wretched conditions under brutal regimes. However, Australia was also a land of opportunity and at least 100 men elected to stay rather than return to Devon at the end of their duty.

The Devonshires also served in Afghanistan between 1879 and 1880 and in South Africa during the Boer War of 1899 to 1902.

World War I

Following the outbreak of the Great War the village's young men began volunteering for military service in significant numbers. From 1916 they were forced to join the army or navy through conscription and although the Devonshires had two cyclist battalions which remained in the UK, a number of troops from Parracombe were dispatched overseas. They exchanged the tranquility of Exmoor for the worst scenes of carnage ever known on a modern battlefield.

According to the granite war memorial in the grounds of Christchurch, Parracombe lost eight young men during the Great War. The first to appear on the memorial plaque in Christchurch was also the first Parracombe man listed to die in action. Edwin James Antell was a leading stoker aboard the old-style battleship HMS Goliath. He died, aged 40, on 13th May 1915 when his ship was sunk in the Mediterranean, after being torpedoed.

Of the 750 crew fewer than 250 were saved. Edwin, a naval reservist when war broke out, was the son of Mr and Mrs Edwin Antell of Headnacott, Parracombe. They had already lost four children aged five months, three, 14 and 26, and the grief that touched the Antell family can only be imagined. It was further heightened by the death from influenza of Edwin's mother, Sylvia Antell, in the year of the armistice, 1918.

As a teenager in Parracombe Edwin had been a servant to William Lock, of East Bodley, who himself died before the war ended, shortly before the death of his only son (also called William - see below). Edwin was married to Annie, with one child, and is remembered on his wife's gravestone, which stands just a few feet from the Christchurch memorial. His name also appears on a family tombstone at St Petrock's and the Naval Memorial at Plymouth Hoe.

William James Henry Lang, a private in the Devonshire Regiment who died on 25th September 1915, was the only child of James and Jane Lang, of Lorna Doone Cottage, Churchtown. Known as Harry, he was just 21 years old. He fell on the first day of a failed offensive at Loos in France and was last seen alive charging German trenches.

John Leworthy, another private in the Devonshires, is also listed on Parracombe's war memorial although his father is recorded as living at Molland Cross, North Molton. He died on 2nd February 1916, aged 19, and is buried in Plymouth, having served in the UK throughout the conflict. A link with Parracombe is believed to have been forged through the Wesleyan Chapel Sunday School.

Tragically, two of the men on the war memorial died within 24 hours of one another, just weeks before the war ended. William Lock, a private in the Royal Devon and Royal North Devon Yeomanry (a battalion of the Devonshire Regiment) died in France on 2nd September 1918, aged 26, having spent most of the war serving in the army. He was the son of Betsy and the late William Lock of East Bodley in Parracombe, mentioned previously.

Willie, as he was known, had already seen action in the Dardanelles and Palestine before his death in France and had been wounded twice. Just weeks before his death he had been home to Parracombe, presumably to visit his recently widowed mother. She had lost her husband, a member of Barnstaple Rural District Council and the Board of Guardians, in March after a fall. Later she gave a sacrament glass to Parracombe Methodist Chapel in memory of her son.

The Boys Brigade 1909/1910.

Private Walter Nicholls, who died aged 25 on 1st September 1918 at Arras in France, was in 190 Battalion of the Canadian Expeditionary Force. He had emigrated to Canada with his elder brother in 1911 and enlisted at Winnipeg in Manitoba on 14th November 1916. From his military papers, we know he was born in Martinhoe, gave his occupation as 'farmer', stood nearly six ft tall with dark brown hair and a dark complexion and was a Methodist by faith. He was single and gave his next-of-kin as his father, James Nicholls, of Martinhoe, Parracombe.

Early in 1917 he spent 18 days in a Winnipeg hospital suffering from mumps. But he recovered in time to take passage aboard the SS Justicia on 3rd May 1917 bound from Halifax to Liverpool. By 13th September that year he was seeing action in France.

In November Walter was taken to a field hospital suffering from myalgia, or muscle pain. However this respite from the terrible battlefield conditions lasted a mere four days and records show that by the early summer of 1918 he was dead. In a will written at the end of January 1917 he left everything to his mother, Mary Anne Nicholls of Parracombe.

Canadian papers reveal that Mary was in receipt of Walter's army pay throughout his service in France. Her address is given as Birch Cottage, Parracombe, although it seems more likely that this property was actually in Martinhoe. Walter, together with William Lock and John Leworthy, are also remembered on a plaque at the Methodist Church in Lynton.

Henry John Rottenbury, son of Mrs Fanny Rottenbury of Parracombe whose wedding celebrations have been descibed previously, was a lance corporal in the Royal Warwickshire Regiment when he died on 26th July, 1915 aged 21; a victim of the ill-fated Gallipoli campaign in Turkey. According to news reports, his death was caused by dysentery. After growing up in Parracombe, where he was the village band's euphonium player, Henry worked for Coventry Corporation Tramways but often returned to spend holidays with his widowed mother. Newspaper reports say he'd visited her just a month before his death.

Mrs Rottenbury had another son, a private in the Devonshire Regiment, while her brother Mr E Wood was in the Army Service Corps. One sad footnote to Henry's death is that his replacement as euphonium player in the village band, William Holding, also died in the conflict (see below).

Frederick Edward Walters was a sergeant in the Australian Infantry when he was killed in France on 3rd September 1916, aged 35. He was the youngest son of Thomas and Elizabeth Walters of Prisonford, Parracombe and there's a memorial headstone dedicated to them all in the old churchyard. Thomas had been born in North Petherton while Elizabeth came from Combe Martin. Sgt Walters was the last of their ten children; the others were Lucy, Thirza, Sabrina, Mary, Bessie, Thomas, William, John and George.

Frederick served with the 4th Voluntary Battalion of the Devonshire Regiment for eight years before emigrating to Australia. The date he left North Devon for the Antipodes is unknown although it was probably sometime between 1910 and 1914. However we do know that he turned up at a recruiting centre for the Australian Army in Blackboy Hill, Western Australia, soon after the outbreak of the First World War. Australian military records list him as a timber worker, five ft six ins (1.68 m) tall, weighing 148 lbs (67.3 kg) with dark complexion, brown eyes and dark hair. He belonged to the Church of England and had a Union Jack tattooed on his forearm.

From Australia as a member of the 11th Battalion, 3rd Infantry Brigade of the Australian Imperial Force, Frederick travelled to Egypt and then to the Gallipoli Peninsula. During that ill-conceived campaign against Turkish troops he received gunshot wounds to his right arm and was hospitalized in Alexandria. He returned to duty but was later re-admitted for three weeks suffering from a fever. Eventually he was posted back to Gallipoli for six months before his battalion withdrew to Egypt.

In June 1916 Frederick sailed for Europe and the Somme. He survived some of the heaviest fighting of the war and during the height of battle on 18th August was promoted twice on the same day, first to corporal; then sergeant, reflecting the massive losses sustained by Australian forces. Within three weeks of his arrival in the Somme he was dead, aged just 35. Although he has no known grave his name is carved on the Australian memorial at Villiers-Bretonneux - along with some 11,000 others who fell in battle.

Details of the final name on the memorial, J. Somerwill, are unclear although we know that a Corporal Lewis W. Somerwill, of the Royal Engineers, won a Military Medal at Ypres in 1917. He was the son of George Somerwill of Parracombe. Neither is it clear why the name of two other Parracombe men who died - William Holding and Samuel Sharp - are mentioned on a roll of honour inside the church but not on the memorial cross.

Our research places William Holding in the Royal West Kents. A veteran of the Boer War, he was a lance corporal when he died at Ypres on 17th December 1914 after being struck on the head by a shell. Married with one son, he had been a member of the Parracombe Brass Band before leaving the area for Tunbridge Wells about a year before he enlisted. He is known to have returned to the village in June, shortly before the outbreak of the First World War. Research into the story of Samuel Sharp has so far produced no results.

Memorial mystery

There are records of other servicemen with Parracombe connections who died in the First World War and, once again, it is unclear why their names do not appear on the war memorial. The youngest son of Mrs Wallis of Parracombe, a member of the Australian Imperial Force, died on the same day as Frederick Walters while Rupert Randolph Winter, a flight commodore in the pioneering Royal Navy Air Service, died on 3rd February 1918 aged 21. His parents were listed at addresses in Parracombe and London and were the last couple to wed in St Petrock's church until 2003. Edward Ducarel Palmer had a Parracombe address when he enlisted in a London regiment. He was a 20 year old lance corporal when he died on 30th October 1917. His parents, Sir Frederick and Lady Palmer, lived in Coleford, Gloucestershire.

Frederick West Bristow, a veteran of the Boer War, was killed on 18th July 1916, aged 46, while serving with a Welsh Regiment. He was the son of the late Richard Bristow and Mary Ann Ridd (formerly Bristow), of Martinhoe Farm. His half brother S Ridd lost a leg and was taken prisoner by the Germans but returned home after the war ended.

The roll of honour inside the church records the names of 58 who served and survived. It reveals that no fewer than eight of the Antell family fought against Germany. Research shows that Fred and Edwin were brothers, as were Arthur and Sidney. The others - George, Henry, Abel and Percy - were probably their second cousins. The Antell family originally came from Dorset and Somerset and turned up in Parracombe and Challacombe in the middle of the 19th century. Parracombe seems to be populated with the descendants of James Antell, born in Maperton, Somerset, and his wife Grace, from Stalbridge in Dorset, both of whom died in Parracombe. They had three sons and two daughters (including Martha Hawkes - see Making of a Village) who between seem to have given the couple no fewer than 26 grandchildren and possibly even more. However, many died at a tragically early age.

Fred Antell served on HMS Warspite and later had his daughter baptized Sylvia Warspite Antell. When he returned from the war he resumed his job as a village postman, using pony power to undertake his rounds. On 9th January 1941 the North Devon Journal and Herald recorded his retirement as follows:

'Mr F Antell, probably the only official mounted postman over a very wide area has retired from the postal service at Parracombe and has been the subject of a presentation. He retired on 29th December and a pleasant little ceremony took place at the office on 1st January when Mr Cooke, a retired Post Office official, presented him with a case of pipes and a tobacco pouch subscribed for by Miss Crocombe, late post mistress and Mr A Parkhouse, present sub postmaster, and staff of Parracombe post office as a token of the esteem in which he has been held over the whole of his 33 years service. Mr Antell suitably responded. He will be remembered as being postman in the Challacombe district and later became the only officially mounted postman travelling to Woody Bay on a pony.'

Meanwhile Arthur Antell won the Military Medal for gallantry in the field during service with the 2nd Battalion, the Coldstream Guards. He had stayed with an injured senior officer under fire during the Battle at Ypres in October 1916 and although the man subsequently died of his injury his mother never forgot Arthur's bravery. She later presented him with her son's gold watch, appropriately inscribed. Arthur is buried with his brother Sydney at Christchurch. Another Military Medal holder was Private A Kinsey of Lorna Doone, Parracombe, honoured in 1918, and a second Antell, George, was awarded the Distinguished Service Medal.

One of the most dramatic war stories involving a son of Parracombe concerned that of J Cooke (another postman). He escaped with his life following the sinking of the cruiser HMS Hawke by a German submarine in the North Sea. He was among just 21 survivors from a crew of 550.

The attack in October 1914 was reported in the North Devon Journal: 'About 11 am the periscope of a submarine was observed, shortly afterwards the cruiser was struck and subsequently the submarine rose from cover to see the effect of her discharge, disappearing immediately afterwards beneath the waters. The Hawke keeled over, which prevented the gunners from firing at the sub. There was an explosion which shook the vessel violently and she settled down within eight minutes.

'Mr Cooke on the main deck plunged into the icy water and after swimming about three quarters of a mile was picked up by a cutter, the only boat which had been able to get away from the doomed ship.'

Cooke was among 49 people aboard on a small boat designed for many fewer people. They were tossed about in heavy seas for five hours before a Norwegian steamer came to the rescue and transferred them a trawler. They were eventually landed at Aberdeen.

William Nicholls, brother of the ill-fated Walter, was a farm labourer in Canada when he was drafted in November 1917. At 34 he was some ten years older than his sibling, five feet eight inches tall, with black hair and hazel eyes. He bore a scar on the palm of his left hand. Another Methodist, he also listed their father James, of Parracombe, as his next-of-kin.

Parracombe servicemen wounded in the war included Richard Couch, W. Tamlyn, Richard Poole, Frank Smith, Bert Hoyles, F. Chugg, Thomas Crocombe, Fred Bray, C Watts and John Blackmore.

Life in Parracombe was largely unaffected by the distant war, although there were constant reminders of its existence. Children were encouraged to search Chapman Barrows for young and tender fox gloves which could be dried in the Malt House and dispatched to provide medical ingredients that would in turn aid injured soldiers. In 1916 there was tremendous excitement when an airplane flew over the school, a sight never seen before. In these pre-Royal Air Force days British air power consisted of the Royal Flying Corps and the Royal Navy Air Corps. The RFC had just 179 aircraft at the outbreak of the First World War and most were in action on the Western Front.

On one occasion schoolchildren were allowed to stand at Bodley Cross to cheer soldiers marching out of Lynton (it was, of course, years before the bypass and all traffic passed directly through Parracombe.) Another stark reminder of the war occurred in 1918 when a large gun was towed through the village. Throughout the conflict villagers raised money from whist drives to buy Christmas gifts for soldiers and residents collectively contributed 3,663 eggs between 1916 and 1919 to help nourish the wounded - part of a regional welfare campaign organised by Barnstaple's mayoress. By 1918 conscription was taking its toll on the village and crops were sown late as farmers struggled to survive a labour shortage.

World War II

I said to the man who stood at the gate of the year
Give me a light that I may tread safely into the unknown
And he replied, go out into the darkness and put your hand into the hand of God
That shall be to you better than light
And safer than a known way
So I went forth and finding the Hand of God
Trod gladly into the night
And he led me towards the hills
And the breaking of the day in the lone East

Minnie Louise Harkins, quoted by King George VI in his Christmas broadcast of 1939.

In Parracombe - as in every other town and village across Britain - families sat huddled around the radio that Christmas; listening to the King's words, mindful of the British Expeditionary Force in France, perhaps mouthing a prayer for its deliverance and always, always, wondering about talk of a German invasion. In one sense the war was far removed; in another it was uncomfortably close. Out in the Bristol Channel and the Atlantic beyond, the U-boat packs were busy. The future had never seemed more uncertain.

Although Parracombe remained out of the direct firing line villagers heard the waves of German night bombers seeking industrial targets across in South Wales. One of these enemy planes crash-landed at Martinhoe Common. Arthur Parkhouse, from the Old Post Office, was among many on the scene. He, helped by others arrested a crewman who had parachuted to safety. The prisoner was escorted back to Parracombe and held until army personnel arrived.

On another occasion a bomb fell on Higher Holwell, Parracombe, behind what was then the home of Wallace Leworthy. It was probably jettisoned by a German pilot acting to lighten his load as he tried to escape a pursuing British fighter. The house at Higher Holwell is now in ruins.

Emma Worth and Tom Daborn who were married in Christchurch, Parracombe in 1942. Due to rationing they had to make do with a chocolate wedding cake.

Parracombe home guard 1938 to 1945.

The village had its own Home Guard, operating out of a modest hut at the Pleasure Ground. Members armed with shotguns used to patrol Chapman Barrows on horseback starkly aware of the threat of a German invasion along the North Devon coast. Early in the conflict 40-gallon barrels filled with stones were placed on Chapman Barrows and the Home Guard had orders to up-end them at the first sign of a sea-borne attack, the aim being to thwart any enemy tank advance.

Despite its remote location the war touched every aspect of Parracombe life. First Aid practices were organised in the village by the district nurse, with 'victims' scattered on the roads with fake injuries for trainees to identify and treat. Local men and boys supplemented their income by hunting rabbits for a butcher who visited the village regularly. Sometimes city dwellers came to stay in Parracombe with a similar purpose in mind.

Like everywhere else Parracombe became an extended vegetable patch. During the early years of the war, when Germany had the upper hand, the prospect of Britain being starved into submission seemed very real as ships bringing supplies from across the Atlantic were regularly sunk by the U-boats.

As a result, children were given time off school to pick potatoes and other crops needed both locally and nationally. Farmer John Petherick, a pupil at Parracombe School between the ages of six and 14, also recalls farmers being told what to plant as part of the national cultivation effort.

'You had a little book with the day when you were picking potatoes at different farms,' he said. 'We used to go to Martinhoe to do the Dallyns. We went by horse and cart very often. It was hard lifting up the buckets and bags all day long.

'There was generally a man with a boy. The boy held on to the bag and the man chucked in the potatoes. The small potatoes were pulped for cattle. They ate them raw with oats on the top. The rest went off for human consumption.'

Prior to the outbreak of the Second World War, Parracombe Parish Council was asked to undertake a house-to-house survey for the Government Evacuation scheme. Parish councillors decided that all their efforts were being devoted to the Air Raid Precaution training and that it would be impossible to carry out the request. They passed it to the local branch of the Women's Institute. Another letter received in the spring of 1939 asked councillors to outline what mortuary accommodation existed in the village. It was decided that Mr Creech would, in an emergency, provide a garage under the local ARP First Aid Station to be used for bodies if necessary.

By 1940, Parracombe's war effort was in full swing. On Empire Day (24th May 1940) schoolchildren collected 12s 9d, which was sent to the Overseas League for distribution to 'fighting men'. Old machinery was salvaged from farms and its sale in September 1940 yielded £8 and 8d. After expenses of £1 6s had been paid the remainder was forwarded to the Red Cross. The same year local women collected sticks, whortleberries and blackberries, raising £1 6s 5d from their sale. The money was spent on wool to knit pullovers, scarves and bedsocks for the Red Cross.

Newspaper reports from later in the war record that C F Maddison was summoned before the local court for selling 25 eggs at a price in excess of the maximum laid down in law. Both he and the buyer, C. Blackmore of the Globe Inn, Berrynarbour, were fined 30 shillings.

In August 1940, just weeks before the Blitz was unleashed upon London, a letter from Barnstaple Rural District Council was read to parish councillors asking if Parracombe was now prepared to receive evacuees. A letter was sent back asking how many would arrive. By December there were more than 20 evacuees on the school roll.

In the same year the school's windows were protected by galvanised wire on the advice of the local education authority (the cost was less than £5). Teachers also drew up plans to evacuate the school in the event of an air raid. They were to be taken to the Long Walk leading to Heddon Hall and rehearsals of the evacuation procedure were carried out weekly. This regular practice ensured that the entire school could be emptied inside two minutes.

During War Weapons week in April 1941 parish councillors heard that the school had raised an astonishing £102. At the same meeting councillors discussed the surface at the bottom of Tarr Path, which had led to some complaints from local residents. Given that dark nights were approaching, and the blackout was in force, councillors decided to carry out repairs.

Blackout rules

By December council meetings were held at Mr Delbridge's home because the school had no blackout curtains at its windows. Mr Edwards, responsible for collecting refuse, had asked for a rise of £6 to cover the costs of labour and the increased workload created by the evacuees in the village. After a lengthy discussion a rise of £3 was agreed. Clearly, this did little to mollify Mr Edwards who resigned in the middle of 1943.

Four stirrup pumps for fighting fires, along with steel helmets, were sent to Parracombe by BRDC during the early part of the war. In February 1942 ten volunteers came forward to man the Fire Guard, meeting for practice every Wednesday. Led by Messrs Tossell and Delbridge, the team included Archie Smyth, Dick Smyth, W G and H Crocombe, G Walters, W Leworthy and T Petherick. On Saturday 28th February 1942 parish councillors again toured the village with horse-drawn carts to collect iron and metal salvage. Within a month BDRC had taken away one ton 18 cwts and 3 qrs of scrap metal.

By 8th October that year the villagers had raised £575 for a tank collection, far in excess of their hopes. That year £16 8s 6d was collected in the Poppy Day appeal and a whist drive held in December by the Parracombe and District British Legion raised sufficient funds to ship 33 Christmas

Carvings on a beach tree between Bumsley Mill and the Beacon, 60 years on they can still be read quite easily.

RAF Gosport was, along with Lee-on-Solent, one of the Royal Navy's airfields used in the defence of Southampton and Portsmouth. Royal Navy fighters were permanently based there, and occasionally RAF units were detached, using the airfield in the same way as a satellite or relief landing ground.

gifts to men and women serving overseas.

In March 1945 the following parish council budget was agreed by councillors.

	£	s	d
Clerk's Salary	2		
Postage a/c		3	10
Financial statements and Audit forms (from Harper's)		8	
Cleaning War Memorial (W J Blackmore)		15	
Cleaning school room after two meetings		3	
Total	3	9	10

For those who wrestle with pre-decimal figures, that all adds up to £3.49.

From 1941 there was increasing evidence of military activity around Parracombe. American troops camped at Trentishoe and Ellen or Nell Worth who lived at Mill Farm put the kettle on the Bodley as soon as she heard their footfall on Spoon Path, leading from Trentishoe into the Heddon Valley. The men were treated to a cup of tea and piece of cake as they passed. When she was asked why she showed such hospitality to servicemen she replied: 'I hope someone is doing the same for my two soldier sons, wherever they are.' In fact, she lost a son, Fred, to the war.

Precise troop movements around the village are unknown although it's clear that men from the US Army Air Force, who were billeted in the area, dug at Beacon Quarry for stone to build the runways at Chivenor air base, Barnstaple. Some servicemen left their initials carved in the trees between Bumsley Mill and the Beacon.

The minutes of meetings held by the Buffs during the Second World War provide an important insight into village life at the time. As early as 1936 there's talk of an impending conflict and a meeting 'for the purpose of demonstrating to the people how to carry on in case of gas attack on this country.'

During the war the brothers in the Buffalo order sent cigarettes or five-shilling postal orders to their fellow lodge members serving overseas. Records show that in 1939 the proceeds of a draw were used to send 100 cigarettes to Brother P Blackmore in France. The following spring, copies of the Buff Journal were sent to brethren serving overseas.

In 1942 the ARP warden inspected the Buff Hall's blackout curtains - although there were only a handful of Tilley lamps available to light the building. Sometimes the hall was booked for 'Air Raid Precaution instruction' and although the Home Office paid no rent it did provide a cleaning grant. Records also show that the Hall was used as a billet for soldiers on manoeuvre around Exmoor, and as a reception centre for evacuees.

More frequently though it was the focus of fundraising events. Among the wartime good causes to benefit were the Spitfire Fund, the China Fund, Support for Malta Fund, Salute the Soldier Committee and, later, the Victory Celebration and Welcome Home funds.

On 15th January 1942 the Buffs hosted a party for local children and evacuees, staging conjuring tricks, dancing and games. Misses Ethel Blackmore and E Ridd were in charge and each child was presented with a shilling by the Buffs (five pence in today's money). A week later there was a whist drive and dance at the hall organised by the Parracombe and District branch of the British Legion, which was recouping funds after sending 30 Christmas gifts to local people in the forces. The highlight of March 1944 was a dance featuring a raffle prize of a basket of fruit from Africa - with the promise that it would include a banana.

RAF men who were Brothers at Lodges elsewhere in the country came to meetings and helped with fund raising and social events. The RAF also hired the hall for its own monthly dances. Several airmen corresponded with the Lodge for some time after they moved on.

Minutes of meetings make short references to Parracombe men on active service. In September 1944 Brother Short 'wrote to say how happy he was to be able to tell us that his son was now a prisoner of war in Germany'. According to the minutes, Fred Worth was the only member of the Lodge to die in the conflict (his name does not appear on the village's war memorial). In fact Fred Worth, the son of Nell and James Worth at Mill Farm, came from Shirwell, where he lived with his wife Phyllis. He is remembered in a framed testimonial on the wall inside the Buff Hall.

The Buffs initiated the 'Welcome Home' fund which secured both Parish Council and village support. Money was earmarked for returning servicemen but the perplexing question of who was eligible for what took many hours of debate. Ultimately every candidate was individually assessed before the money was divided up and awarded.

During the war, or soon afterwards, a large container was sent by the residents of Parracombe in Australia containing luxury items like sugar and dried fruit. Australian Rosemary van Dueken remembers her mother, Rena Hurst, transforming their lounge into a packaging plant.

'Everything was transported in hessian bags sewn up with big needles,' she recalled. 'There was egg powder, dried chocolate, sultanas and other items.' Although the gift, dispatched through the postal system, was officially sent from one local school to another the foodstuffs were donated by many different families in Australia.

Before the war was all over, Parracombe had lost three of its young men. Trooper William Frederick Crocombe, whose wife Louisa and parents William and Bessie all lived in the village, served in the 1st Royal Tank Regiment. He was 26 when he died on 10th June 1942 in the Middle East.

Alfred Granville Crompton was another member of the Royal Tank Regiment. Aged 23 when he fell on 10th May 1942, he had lived with his wife Mary in Parracombe, although his parents lived in Combe Martin. Finally there was James Edward Moore, a Royal Marine, who was 28 when he died on 5th July 1941. He was the son of James and Helena Moore, then living in Barnstaple.

One sad footnote to Parracombe's war years occurred after hostilities ceased when a Spitfire crashed on Clement's Hill near the village, killing the pilot. The wreckage remained there for years afterwards.

The most recent name on the War Memorial is that of Richard Barton, a private in the Parachute Regiment, who died during the Troubles in Northern Ireland on 14th July 1971, aged 24. According to the Paras' internal records Private Barton, who lived at The Ark, Parracombe, was shot on patrol in Anderstown, Belfast, as he drove at gunmen to cover his colleagues. He was just two months away from his wedding. It was 20 years before the name was added to the memorial following a campaign by villagers.

The names on Parracombe's war memorial are:

1914-18
E J Antell
W J H Lang
J Leworthy
W Lock
W Nicholls
H Rottenbury
J Somerwill
F Walters

1939-1945
W F Crocombe
A E Crompton
J E Moore

1971
R Barton

11 Extremes of Weather

She lit a candle in her bedroom, little realising the catastrophe that was unfolding around her.

The huge mass of earth torn away by the flood south of Parracombe. The embankment was part of the Barnstaple Lynton railway. Much of the water that reached Parracombe came through this gap

It became known around the globe as the Lynmouth Flood; the legacy of a terrible storm which transformed the East and West Lyn rivers into raging torrents and brought death and devastation on an unimaginable scale. The incessant rain also took its toll on neighbouring communities like Parracombe, where complaints about the swamped roads and damp buildings were soon put into dark and tragic perspective.

On the night of 15th August 1952 rainwater which had been building up for days behind the blocked drainage holes of a disused railway culvert finally broke through. Suddenly, the hopelessly swollen River Heddon was surging down through the village, carrying with it a lethal cargo of boulders and trees. The waters swept away 60 year old postman William Leworthy, who had been braving the terrible weather to make sure his sister was safe.

Audrey Petherick, born at East Bodley farm in 1923, recalls that dreadful night. 'There was torrential rain in the area and, because of the downpours, my two brothers Archie and George Smyth, were doing "barn work", making spears to use in thatching the corn ricks.

'Bill Leworthy called in for a chat on his way home from helping Farmer Douglas Ridd with his corn at West Bodley. After a while he left my brothers to their work, saying "I had better brish along homeward". Tragically, that same night he was washed away in the flood, when the railway bank gave way and a torrent of water came rushing down the valley and through Parracombe village.'

Farmer Gilbert Walters was 14 at the time of the flood. 'It was a Friday night and there had been terrrible thunder and rain through the day. The bridge by the school was washed away as well as the one by the pub.

'Most of the damage was caused by the collapse of the old railway embankment just beneath the bypass. The water came down the valley like a tidal wave. Afterwards the river was like a shingle beach and you could see right up the valley, as everything in its path had been cleared. The water covered the gatepost on our farm, a depth of about six ft.'

The school wall and playground was also left damaged by flood water.

At Mill Farm Rosie Rogers had been awoken by the sound of wind, beating rain, falling boulders and paint pots tumbling from the garage shelves. She lit a candle in her bedroom, little realising the catastrophe that was unfolding around her.

That candle proved a life-saving beacon for French schoolboy Anthony Penaud whose nearby holiday chalet had been swept away like matchwood. He found himself terrified and disorientated in the murky water but struck out towards Rosie's flame and managed to clutch a hook above Mill Farm's back door. There he screamed for help.

Rosie swiftly woke her mother, Nell Worth, who tried to get into the kitchen by the back stairs. Horrified, she saw water coming up to meet her and she and Rosie quickly roused a visitor staying at the farm. Using a bed sheet, the visitor helped Rosie's husband Claude pull 14-year-old Anthony - bruised, bleeding and shocked - to safety through a bedroom window.

Anthony was staying with his English penpal Roger Thorn, also 14, and his mother Alys who were from Woking, Surrey. Sadly, Roger and his mother were among those who died in the storm. Anthony went on to become a doctor in Marseilles. He returned to the area several times to say 'thank you' to his rescuers, most recently on the 50th anniversary of the flood in 2002.

The following morning Nell came down the backstairs to find the kitchen awash. A pig stood grunting on the kitchen table. A large tree trunk was firmly wedged across the next room and had to be sawn up before the door could open. The road to Hunter's Inn outside was left covered with dead trout and it took six weeks of cleaning before Mill Farm was habitable again. Claude found his motorbike buried in a shed amongst the rubble. His tractor needed a new engine before it would fire up again and the family car was irrepairable.

That night 34 men, women and children around the region died and some 92 properties were destroyed. The body of one young woman remains unidentified. *[Another body was uncovered by the flood waters at Heddon's Mouth, although it dates from a different era. No one knows the identity of*

Outside the Fox & Goose after the flood in 1952.

The girl by the table is Christine Parker; the three men talking are F R Latham, Harry Smyth and J Edwards; the Policeman is J Gammon talking to H W Hoyles; and the two boys are James and Harold Latham.

the victim; perhaps a shipwrecked sailor or a sea-traveller who perished aboard ship before being brought ashore for burial - Ed.]

Holiday nightmare

One visitor was left counting his blessings. He had come to Parracombe two weeks prior to the flood and crashed into the walls of the Fox & Goose at the bottom of Parracombe Hill. His wife ended up in hospital and a daughter broke her arm. The weather for the remainder of their stay was nothing short of atrocious. But if he thought it could not get any worse, he was wrong. During the flood his van, containing all the family's luggage and his wallet, was washed away. At least he and his relatives lived to tell the tale.

When Prince Philip visited Lynmouth to offer his condolences the staff and children of Parracombe School made their way to the 'new road' bearing hand-made flags to wave at his passing car. A relief fund which collected money from across the world stood at £1,336,425 when it closed in August 1954. It was used to support the 1,740 people hit by the calamity.

There are plenty of other examples of severe weather in Parracombe, including snowfalls that have isolated the village for days at a time. Heavy snowfalls occurred in 1952, 1963, 1978 and 1981.

Bill Delbridge remembers householders ensuring they had a ready supply of canned food in preparation for the annual snowfall. He recalls one winter's day when he and a friend took the family's wireless accumulator (power pack) to be recharged at Barbrook garage. 'We made a sledge and walked all the way to Barbrook. But we couldn't get home because of the snow. We had to stay out there with family friends for three days before we could get back to Parracombe.

'When I was in the army in 1947 I visited Parracombe and it snowed so hard I could not get out of the village again. The council employed me to clear snow. I worked with Italian prisoners of war to clear clear a path through the village. I don't know where they were stationed though.'

The village bathed in splendid weather as well. In August 1899 a newspaper report tells of a hot spell. 'Hay harvest is pretty well over here. The yield is quite up to the average and the hay has been saved in capital condition. Cabbages on the whole have been rather a failure. Rape and grass vary. Rooks, which are getting very numerous, have done considerable damage. Straw is rather short and mangold and turnips vary. Rain is badly needed.'

Other drowning tragedies have also occurred in and around Parracombe. In 1889 Parracombe farmer Richard Gammin drowned himself in Pinkery Pond. A keen cricketer, he lived at Rowley Barton and farmed more than 1,000 acres. When his wife Emma died aged 38 in 1882 he was left with 10 children to raise.

Shortly before his death the 48 year old had begun a relationship with a local woman. However, her decision that they should part apparently led to his suicide. On Wednesday 13th March 1889 he visited the Fox & Goose, announcing his intentions to drown himself.

After Gammin went missing his clothes were discovered by the pond's shore. The following day the captain of Lynmouth Lifeboat, John Crocombe, took a boat to Pinkery Pond to drag the water but no body was found.

A diver from Cardiff was subsequently called in and dynamite was set off in the water to dislodge the body, believed to be trapped below the surface. All efforts failed until Bob Jones, the man who designed Lynton's Cliff Railway and built the Foreland Lighthouse, was called in. Using spars and jacks he forced out a pipeline plug to drain the pond. Gammin's body was found close to where he had left his clothes.

In the pocket of his waistcoat was the letter from the woman finishing the relationship. The activities caused an enormous stir with 1,000 people visiting Pinkery Pond on the Sunday before the body was found.

An inquest decided Gammin committed suicide while temporarily insane. He is buried with his wife in the old church, along with two daughters. Agnes Sloley died in 1893 aged 24 and Bessie Gammin died in 1914 aged 35.

John Crocombe was also called on to recover the body of one Mr Wyatt drowned at Woolhanger. The 84 year old, a guest of Sir Henry Palk Carew, apparently slipped and fell into the ornamental pond as he tried to get into a boat, intending to paint an island summerhouse. A verdict of accidental drowning was recorded following an inquest held at Woolhanger Manor.

The remains of the road at Mill Farm in the Heddon Valley, soon after the flood.

On 11th February 1978 a fierce snowstorm started on a Saturday lunchtime and had cut the village off by late afternoon. The snow drifted accross the roads to depths of 15 feet or more, making any kind of access by road quite impossible.

The big chill

Snow began falling on Parracombe during Boxing Day 1962 and continued until drifts were as high as the tops of telegraph poles. Like other villages across North Devon, cut off by road for several weeks, Parracombe received deliveries of bread by helicopter. Secondary school children had an unexpected holiday lasting several weeks.

In 1978 another heavy fall of snow paralysed the village. Powerful winds caused immense drifts in excess of 15 ft.

Local vet Murray Gibson at Laurel House collected some milk on behalf of families with small children. When Bruce Aiken set off from his home, Evenlode, to fetch supplies for his eight month old daughter Lucy, he lost his way in a blinding blizzard.

Later he borrowed a sledge from Helen and Robert Young at Orchardside to slide over frozen fields to Mill Farm in the Heddon Valley to get more milk and eggs. Of course, he then faced an uphill journey but broke just a single egg in the process.

Three years later and Parracombe was hit by a freak wind that flattened a sizeable chunk of the Heddon Valley wood. Afterwards the area resembled a First World War battlefield.

The cold weather returned with a vengeance in 1984 when ice clung to hedges, telegraph poles and electrical transformers. Parracombe was left without power in the five days leading up to Christmas and for a similar length of time after the holiday.

On 12th December 1981 a freak wind storm ran up the Heddon Valley. Within minutes it had taken down trees which had been growing along Spoon Path, on the south side of the valley, for over 100 years. With them went the carved initials of generations of courting couples.

Index

Entries in bold italic refer to illustrations

Printed in Poland
by Amazon Fulfillment
Poland Sp. z o.o., Wrocław

89835620R00056